MAKING GAMES FOR THE ATARI 2600

An 8bitworkshop Book

by Steven Hugg

Making Games for the Atari 2600

Disclaimer

Trademarks

Inquiries

Please refer all inquiries to info@8bitworkshop.com.

Contents

List of Figures

List of Tables

Preface

Like many American kids in 1979, I woke up to find that Santa had left a brand new Atari VCS[1] under the tree (thanks, Mom and Dad, for paying Santa's invoice!). This was a pretty big deal for a six-year-old who could tell you the location and manufacturer of every standup arcade cabinet within a five mile radius. Having an "arcade in your home" wasn't just a thing you saw on *Silver Spoons*, it was now a real thing.

The sights and sounds that jumped off of our little Panasonic color TV probably deserve a gigantic run-on sentence worthy of Dylan Thomas, as my brother and I bounced tiny pixellated missiles off of walls in *Combat*, combed through the perplexing game modes of *Space Invaders*, battled angry duck-like dragons in *Adventure*, and became *Superman* as we put flickering bad guys in a flickering jail. These cartridges were opaque obelisks packaged in boxes with fantastically unattainable illustrations, available at K-Mart for $30 or so.

You could tell these species of video games weren't related to arcade games, though they had a unique look-and-feel of their own. We also had an Apple][by this time, so I tried to fit all of these creatures into a digital taxonomy. Atari games had colors and fast motion, but not as much as arcade games, and they never were as complex as Apple][games. What made them tick? Why were Activision games so much more detailed? Would the missile still blow up your spaceship if you turned the TV off? (Turns out the answer is yes.)

---

[1] It wasn't sold as "Atari 2600" until 1982. We'll use "VCS" in this book, which stands for Video Computer System.

An Atari 2600 four-switch "wood veneer" version, dating from
1980-1982 (photo by Evan Amos)

Soon afterwards, I would start dissecting the Apple][, and never really got my mitts on the viscera inside those VCS cartridges. It wasn't until the Internet came around that I'd discover the TIA chip, scanlines, and emulators like Stella. I'd also read about the people who wrote the games, often uncredited, who pushed the envelopes of both game design and technology while working solo against impossible deadlines.

It's now been 37 years since that Christmas morning, and thanks to the Web, very fast modern CPUs, and lots of open-source sharing, you can program Atari VCS games in your browser. It's probably the most effort you can expend for the fewest number of pixels, but it's also really rewarding.

If the modern software ecosystem is a crowded and bureaucratic megalopolis, programming the VCS is like tinkering in a tiny cabin in the woods with 10-foot snow drifts outside. At least the stove is working, and there's plenty of wood. Enjoy.

1

Introduction to 6502

In 1974, Chuck Peddle was a Motorola employee trying to sell their 6800 microprocessor to customers for $300 each. He and a few co-workers left the company with the vision of a much cheaper alternative, and landed at MOS Technology in Valley Forge, Pennsylvania.

They began drawing the layout for the chip on a huge sheet of paper in one of the offices. Later, they'd cut the table-sized Rubylith photomask for the 3,510 transistors by hand, wearing clean socks so they wouldn't damage the mask when they had to step over something. The design (mostly) worked on the first run, and the 6502 was sold out of large jars for $25 at the 1975 Wescon trade show.[1] It would sell tens of millions of units over the next decade.

The 6502 CPU was not that much different from other micro-processors in function; it was just cheap and widely available. Yet it powered the Apple I and Apple][computers, the Com-modore 64, the Nintendo Entertainment System, and the Atari 2600/VCS, as well as a myriad of other computers and game devices.

While there are plenty of books and online resources devoted to 6502 programming, we're going to cover the basics in this chapter before we jump straight into programming the Atari 2600. Feel free to skip to the next chapter if you already know most of this stuff; we won't cover VCS-specific topics until Chapter Two.

1.1 Bits, Bytes, and Binary

All digital computers operate on bits and bytes and, on the VCS, you'll be manipulating them directly. Let's review a few things about them.

A bit is a binary value – it can be either zero (0) or one (1). A byte is a sequence of eight bits.

We can create a written representation of a byte in *binary notation*, which just lists the bits from left to right, for example: %00011011. We can then shorten the byte notation by removing the leading zeros, giving us %11011. The % denotes a binary number, and we'll use this notation throughout the book.

The eight bits in a byte are not just independent ones and zeros; they can also express numbers. We assign values to each bit and then add them up. The least-significant bit, the rightmost (our index starts at zero, i.e. *bit 0*), has a value of 1. For each position to the left, the value increases by a power of two until we reach the most-significant bit, the leftmost (*bit 7*) with a value of 128. Here are the values for an entire byte:

Bit #	7	6	5	4	3	2	1	0
Value	128	64	32	16	8	4	2	1

Let's line up our example byte, %11011, with these values:

Bit #	7	6	5	4	3	2	1	0
Value	128	64	32	16	8	4	2	1
Our Byte	0	0	0	1	1	0	1	1
Bit*Value				16	8		2	1

When we add up all the bit values, we get $16 + 8 + 2 + 1 = 27$.

1.2 Hexadecimal Notation

Binary notation can be unwieldy, so it's common to represent bytes using *hexadecimal notation*, or *base 16*. We split the byte into two 4-bit halves, or *nibbles*. We treat each nibble as a separate value from 0 to 15, like this:

Bit #	7	6	5	4	3	2	1	0
Value	8	4	2	1	8	4	2	1

Table 1.1: Bit Values in Hexadecimal Notation

We then convert each nibble's value to a symbol – 0-9 remains 0 through 9, but 10-15 becomes A through F.

Let's convert the binary number %11011 and see how it would be represented in hexadecimal:

Bit #	7	6	5	4	3	2	1	0
Value	8	4	2	1	8	4	2	1
Our Byte	0	0	0	1	1	0	1	1
Bit*Value				1	8		2	1
Decimal Value	1				11			
Hex Value	1				B			

Table 1.2: Example Hex Conversion

We see in Table 1.2 that the decimal number 27, represented as %11011 in binary, becomes $1B in hexadecimal format. (The $ prefix indicates a hexadecimal number.)

1.3 Signed vs. Unsigned Bytes

One more thing about bytes: We've described how they can be interpreted as any value from 0 through 255, or an *unsigned* value. We can also interpret them as negative or *signed* quantities.

This requires a trick known as *two's complement* arithmetic. If the high bit is 1 (in other words, if the unsigned value is 128 or greater), we treat the value as negative, as if we had subtracted 256 from it:

```
0-127 ($00-$7F):      positive
128-255 ($80-$FF):    negative (value - 256)
```

Note that there's nothing in the byte identifying it as signed – it's all in how you interpret it, as we'll see later.

Now that we know what bits and bytes are, let's see how the CPU manipulates them.

1.4   The CPU and the Bus

Think of the CPU as an intricate timepiece. An electronic spring unwinds and an internal clock ticks 1.19 million times per second. On every tick, electrons turn tiny gears, and the CPU comes to rest in a different state. Each tick is called a *clock cycle*, or *CPU clock*, and you'll learn to become aware of their passing as you learn how to program the VCS.

All the CPU does is execute instructions, one after another, in a fetch-decode-execute cycle. It fetches an instruction (reads it from memory), decodes it (figures out what to do) and then executes it (does some things in a prescribed order). Each instruction may take several clock cycles to execute, each clock cycle performing a specific step. The CPU then figures out which instruction to grab next, and repeats the process. The CPU keeps the address of the next instruction in a 16-bit register called the *Program Counter (PC)*.

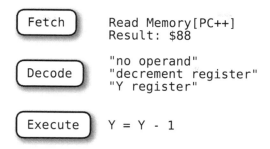

Figure 1.1: CPU Cycle

During each clock cycle, the CPU can read from or write to the bus. The bus is a set of "lanes" where each lane can hold a single bit at a time. The 6502 is an 8-bit processor, so the *data bus* is eight bits (one byte) wide.

Devices like memory and graphics chips are attached to the bus, and receive read and write signals. The CPU doesn't know which devices are connected to the bus – all it knows is that it either receives eight bits back from a read, or sends eight bits out into the world during a write.

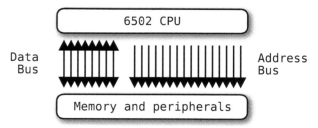

Figure 1.2: Bus

Besides the 8-bit data bus, the 6502 has a 16-bit *address bus*. The address bus describes "where" and the data bus describes "what."

Let's look at what happens when the CPU executes this example instruction, LDA (LoaD A):

```
lda $1234
```

5

The CPU will set the pins on the address bus to the binary encoding for $1234, set the read/write pin to "read," and wait for a response on the data bus. Devices on the bus look at the address $1234 and determine whether the message is for them – by design, only one device should respond. The CPU then reads the value from the data bus and puts it in the A register.

Let's say we are executing the STA instruction (STore A):

```
sta $1234
```

The CPU will set the address bus to $1234 and the data bus to whatever is in the A register, then set the read/write pin to "write." Again, the bus devices look at the address bus and the write signal and decide if they should listen or ignore it. Let's say a memory chip responds – the memory chip would read the 8-bit value off the data bus and store it in the memory cell corresponding to address $1234. The CPU does not get a response from a write; it just assumes everything worked out fine.

You'll note that both of these instructions operate on the A register. The 6502 has three general-purpose registers: A, X, and Y. These are all 8-bit variables that you can manipulate at will. You'll often have to use the registers as temporary storage, for instance: Load a constant value into A, then store A to a given address.

You'll notice that the CPU instructions have a three-letter format. This is called a *mnemonic,* and it's part of the human-readable language used by the CPU, called *assembly language.* The CPU doesn't understand this, but it understands a compact code called *machine code.* A program called an *assembler* takes the human-readable assembly code and produces machine code.

Let's take another example instruction:

```
lda $1234 -> ad 34 12
```

The machine code for this instruction is three bytes, $ad, $34, and $12. $ad is the *opcode* which identifies the instruction and addressing mode. $34 and $12 are part of the *operand*, which in this case is a 16-bit number spanning two bytes. You'll note that the $34 is first and the $12 is second – this is because the 6502 is a *little-endian* processor, expecting the least-significant parts of multibyte quantities first.

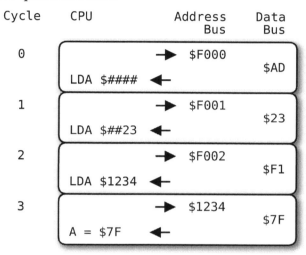

Figure 1.3: LDA Cycle

1.5 Writing Loops

Now we're ready to write a program. Typically, we'd start with the classic example that prints "Hello, World" on the display, but we don't have a display yet! The equivalent program on the Atari 2600 would require us to define the bitmaps for all of the letters in "Hello, World" and we'd also need to learn how CRTs work. So we'll start with something simpler: a loop that counts from 100 (decimal) down to zero.

```
        ldy #100      ; Y = 100
Loop    dey           ; subtract 1 from Y
        bne Loop      ; repeat until Y == 0
```

Here we have three instructions and one label named Loop. In our dialect of 6502 assembler (DASM), instructions are always indented, and labels are always flush against the left margin. Labels can be on their own line or coexist with an instruction. Comments are denoted with a ";" and go until the end of the line.

The first instruction LDY (LoaD Y) loads the Y register with a constant value, 100. Constants start with a "#" and tell the assembler to use the value directly, not as a memory-load or memory-store instruction.

The next instruction DEY (DEcrement Y) subtracts 1 from the Y register. It also sets the Zero (Z) flag in the CPU, which is an internal bit that is set to 1 if the result of an instruction is zero. We use these *flags* to test for conditions in the code.

The final instruction BNE (Branch Not Equal) is a branch in-struction, which means the next instruction may be one of two choices. BNE transfers control to its target label if the Z flag is unset, and will fall through to the next instruction if it is set. In our case, since DEY just set the Z flag, the branch will be taken until the Y register decreases to zero, and so the loop will repeat 100 times.

Let's make a loop that uses the different *addressing modes* of the 6502. These allow you to target areas of memory beyond a single constant location, by adding another register to an address. For example, this demonstrates the *absolute indexed* addressing mode with the STA instruction:

```
        lda #0          ; A <- 0
        ldy #$7F        ; Y <- 127
Loop    sta $100,y      ; store A in [$100+y]
        dey             ; decrement Y, set flags
        bne Loop        ; repeat until Y == 0
```

This loop makes use of two registers, A and Y. A is initialized to zero and Y counts down from $7F (127) to zero. The STA (STore Accumulator) instruction stores A to an address at every loop iteration. We use the addressing mode "absolute,indexed" here, which means we compute the destination address by adding a register (Y in this case) to a constant ($100 in this case). Since Y counts from $7F down to zero, we'll store A (which we set to 0) to addresses $17F to $101 in decreasing order.

In 6502 parlance, the *absolute indexed* mode means add an 8-bit value (Y register in this case) to a 16-bit constant. There is another mode, *zero page* mode, which operates only on 8-bit values. Zero page refers to the memory locations $00-$FF which get special treatment. Instructions using zero-page addressing modes generate smaller code, and most of the VCS registers live in zero-page space.

There are restrictions to these modes, and all combinations do not have a corresponding encoding. For example, only X and Y can be used as indices, the A register cannot be used as an index. Also, Y can only be used as a zero-page index with the LDX and STX instructions – otherwise it is expanded to an absolute index. Your assembler will throw an error if you try to use an invalid addressing mode.

Our last loop has a problem, though. We used the BNE instruction to repeat the loop until Y is zero. But since the store happens *before* we decrement Y, we don't store anything when Y is zero (i.e. at address $100). To fix this, we just change the loop so that the DEY happens before the STA, and add 1 to the starting Y value:

```
        lda #0
        ldy #$80        ; Y <- 128
Loop    dey             ; set flags
        sta $100,y      ; does not modify flags
        bne Loop        ; repeat while Y != 0
```

Since STA does not modify any flags, we can DEY first (which does modify flags) and then exit the loop when Y==0 rather than Y<0. There will be lots of opportunities to tweak loops like this for optimal performance, and VCS programming often demands it.

We could also count upwards from zero using the CPY (ComPare Y) instruction:

```
        lda #0
        tay             ; Y <- 0
Loop    sta $100,y
        iny
        cpy #$80        ; set flags as if (Y - 128)
        bne Loop        ; branch until Y == 128
```

The CPY instruction performs a comparison: It subtracts the operand from the Y register and sets flags, but discards the result. So in this example if Y is $80, (Y-$80) will be zero and the Zero flag will be set.

We can also compare the A register with CMP (CoMPare accumulator) and the X register with CPX (ComPare X register).

1.6 Condition Flags and Branching

We've covered the Z (Zero) flag already, but there are others. Here's the list of condition flags you'll be using most often:

Flag	Name	Description
Z	Zero	Set when the result is zero.
N	Negative/Sign	Set when the result is negative (high bit set).
C	Carry	Set when an arithmetic operation wraps and carries the high bit.
V	Overflow	Set when an arithmetic operation overflows; i.e. if the sign of the result changes due to overflow.

Table 1.3: Condition Flags

A lot of instructions just set the Zero and Negative flags, which makes it easy to test for zero values or to test the high bit. The Carry flag is set by compare, add, subtract, and shift operations.

The Overflow bit is less commonly used than the Carry bit, but it's worth explaining the difference between *wrapping* and *overflow*. When we say a value *wraps*, we mean that an operation exceeds the boundaries of its byte and the result is truncated. So if you add $01 to $FF, you'll wrap around to $00.

Overflow is set when the result of a addition or subtraction changes its sign – for example, $40 + $40 = $80 which overflows because $80 is a negative number in two's complement representation. If you are using unsigned numbers, you can generally ignore this flag.

Mnem.	Description	Flag Test	Condition
BNE	Not Equal	Zero clear	A != B
BEQ	Equal	Zero set	A == B
BCC	Carry Clear	Carry clear	A < B (unsigned)
BCS	Carry Set	Carry set	A ≥ B (unsigned)
BMI	Minus	Negative set	A < B (signed)
BPL	Plus	Negative clear	A ≥ B (signed)
BVC		Overflow clear	no signed overflow
BVS		Overflow set	signed overflow
JMP	Jump	—	always taken

Table 1.4: Branch Instructions

The JMP instruction doesn't test any flags but just moves the PC directly to the target. The branch instructions can only modify the PC by -128 to +127 bytes, so for longer distances you'll need JMP.

It's good to memorize the BCC (less than) and BCS (greater than or equal) instructions, since these are used often. Also note that the BPL and BMI instructions are the same for signed quantities, so we could use them to stop when a value goes negative, like this:

```
        lda #0          ; A <- 0
        ldy #$7F        ; Y <- 127
Loop    sta $100,y      ; store A in [$100+y]
        dey             ; decrement Y, set flags
        bpl Loop        ; repeat until signed(Y) < 0
```

Note that this technique would not work if we started with Y = $81 or higher, because the first DEY would result in a negative number, exiting the loop on the first iteration!

1.7 Addition and Subtraction

We've covered DEY, but there is a whole group of instructions that increment (add one) or decrement (subtract one):

```
DEC  -1 from memory location
DEX  -1 from X register
DEY  -1 from Y register
INC  +1 to memory location
INX  +1 to X register
INY  +1 to Y register
```

There's no INC or DEC for the A register, but you can add or subtract the A register to/from another memory location or constant. ADC adds, and SBC subtracts. An example of addition:

```
lda $81 ; load memory location $81 -> A
clc     ; clear carry flag
adc #10 ; add 10 to A
sta $82 ; store A -> memory location $82
```

Note the CLC (Clear Carry Flag) instruction. The ADC instruction adds the Carry flag to the result (0 or 1) so usually it must be cleared before addition. For subtraction, it must be set first using SEC (Set Carry Flag):

```
lda $81 ; load memory location $81 -> A
sec     ; set carry flag
sbc #10 ; subtract 10 from A
sta $82 ; store A -> memory location $82
```

The increment/decrement instructions modify the Negative and Zero flags, while the addition/subtraction additionally modify the Carry flag.

1.8 The Stack

In computing terminology, a *stack* is a list of values that can grow and shrink. You grow the stack by *pushing* a value on top, and shrink by *pulling* a value off the top.

On the 6502, the stack is stored in RAM, and the top of the stack is a memory location stored in the S (Stack pointer) register. It usually starts at $FF.

The PHA instruction pushes the A register to the stack, storing it to the memory location pointed to by S. It then decrements S by 1. We say the stack "grows upward" because the stack pointer decreases as new values are added.

You can retrieve the top value on the stack with the PLA instruction. It first increments S by 1, then reads the location pointed to by S into A.

Another important instruction that uses the stack is JSR. It pushes the Program Counter to the stack, then transfers control to another location, just like a JMP. When the RTS instruction is encountered, the CPU pulls the top address off of the stack and transfers control there. We'll demonstrate this in Chapter 11.

1.9 Logical Operations

The "logical" instructions combine the bits of the A register and the operand, performing a bit (logic) operation on each bit.

AND	A&B	Set bit if A and B are set.
ORA	A|B	Set bit if A or B (or both) are set.
EOR	A^B	Set bit if either A or B are set, but not both (exclusive-or).
BIT	A&B	Same as AND, but just set flags and throw away the result.

Table 1.5: Logical Instructions

For example, let's combine $55 and $f0 with the AND operation:

```
lda #$55
and #$f0
```

For AND, if a bit was set in both the A register and the operand, it'll be set in A after the instruction executes:

```
        $55  01010101
AND     $f0  11110000
- - - - - - - - - - - - - - - - - - - -
        $50  01010000
```

The AND operation is useful for limiting the range of a value. For example, AND #$1F is the same as (A mod 32), and the result will have a range of 0..31.

What if we did an ORA instead?

```
        $55  01010101
ORA     $f0  11110000
- - - - - - - - - - - - - - - - - - - -
        $f5  11110101
```

ORA sets bits if they are set in either A or the operand, i.e. unless they are clear in both.

What about an EOR?

```
        $55  01010101
EOR     $f0  11110000
- - - - - - - - - - - - - - - - - - - -
        $a5  10100101
```

EOR (exclusive-or) is like an OR, except that bits that are set in both A and the operand are cleared. Note that if we do the same EOR twice, we get the original value back.

1.10 Shift Operations

ASL	Shift Left	Shift left 1 bit (multiply by 2), bit 7 → Carry
LSR	Shift Right	Shift right 1 bit (divide by 2), bit 0 → Carry
ROL	Rotate Left	Same as ASL except Carry → bit 0
ROR	Rotate Right	Same as LSR except Carry → bit 7

Table 1.6: Shift and rotate instructions

There is also the family of "shift" operations that move bits left and right by one position within a byte. The bit that is shifted off the edge of the byte (i.e. the high bit for shift left, and the low bit for shift right) gets put into the Carry flag.

The "rotate" operations are similar, but they also shift the previous Carry flag into the other end of the byte. So for rotate left, the Carry flag is copied into the rightmost (low) bit. For rotate right, it's copied into the leftmost (high) bit.

Example of ASL (shift left):

```
lda #$83
asl      ; shift left
```

Result (C means carry flag is set):

```
          $83  10000011
ASL    -> $06  00000110  C
```

Remember that just like decimal notation, we consider the "leftmost" bit to be the most significant. So if we shift left one bit, we are essentially multiplying by 2. If we shift right one bit, we essentially divide by 2, discarding the remainder.

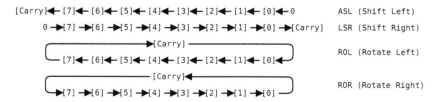

Figure 1.4: Shift and rotate bit flow

Another example, this time of ROR (rotate right):

```
lda #$03
sec        ; set carry flag
ror        ; rotate right
ror        ; rotate right
ror        ; rotate right
```

Note that we SEC to set the carry first. Here's the result:

```
              $03  00000011   C
ROR    ->     $81  10000001   C
ROR    ->     $81  11000000   C
ROR    ->     $81  11100000
```

Note that if you ROL or ROR nine times in succession, you'd have the original byte.

Now that you have a working knowledge of the 6502, we'll use an online tool to program it in the next chapter.

2

The 8bitworkshop IDE

Back in the 1980s, programmers didn't have many tools to help them write games. They certainly didn't have the Internet, and in many cases had to reverse-engineer the VCS themselves! Developers might print out their programs, edit them by hand, then make changes with a cumbersome line editor. Fortunately, we have more efficient tools at our disposal.

In this chapter, we'll discuss the tools we'll use to develop and test our game code. These tools comprise our interactive development environment, or IDE.

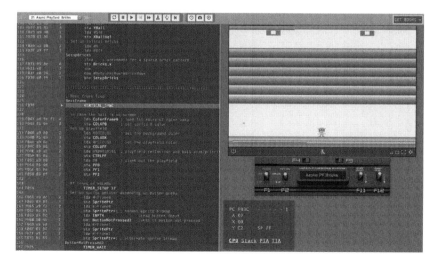

Figure 2.1: 8bitworkshop.com IDE

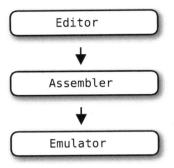

Figure 2.2: IDE Flow

To start the IDE, visit http://8bitworkshop.com/ in a web browser that supports Javascript (for best results, use a recent version of Google Chrome, Mozilla Firefox, or Apple Safari).

The IDE includes an *emulator* which simulates the game console hardware. The emulator we use is called Javatari by Paulo Augusto Peccin[2]. It runs in a web browser, and attempts to simulate the 6502 and all of the VCS hardware cycle-by-cycle as if it were connected to a TV monitor.

The other tool is an *assembler*. The one we use is called DASM[3] and also runs in the web browser, along with a web-based text editor. Each time you make a change to the code, the IDE immediately assembles it and then sends the final ROM image to the VCS emulator, allowing you to see code changes instantly.

The last tool is a simple *debugger* that allows you step through 6502 instructions, view memory, and start and stop the program.

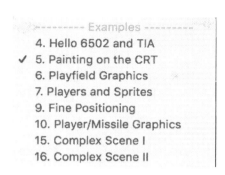

Figure 2.3: IDE Pulldown

The IDE is packaged with several example 6502 assembly files, each roughly corresponding to a chapter in this book. At the top left of the screen, you can access a pulldown menu that allows you to select a file to load. You can edit these files as much as you want – all changes are persisted and they'll be there if you close the browser tab and come back. To reset and fully clear your changes, select **Revert To Original** in the menu.

The buttons at the top of the screen perform several debugging functions:

Figure 2.4: Debugging Functions

- **Reset** - Reset the emulator and start debugging.
- **Pause** - Stop the emulator.
- **Run** - Resume the emulator after pausing.
- **Step** - Execute the next instruction, then stop.
- **Single Frame** - Run until the next video frame starts.
- **Run To Line** - Set a "breakpoint" on the current line (the one the cursor is on). The emulator will stop when execution reaches that instruction.
- **Step Out** - Run until the current subroutine returns.
- **Step** - Go backwards one instruction.
- **Analyze CPU Timing** - This performs a *flow analysis* on your code, computing timing values for each instruction. We'll cover this again in Chapter 40: Timing Analysis.

- **Edit Graphics** - Open graphics editor (not used much in the VCS platform)
- **Start/Stop Replay** - Toggle emulator recording, which lets you replay your game and seek to specific frames.

2.1 Debug Window

Whenever the IDE hits a breakpoint, a debug window appears in the lower-right of the screen. This shows the internal state of the CPU:

- **PC** - Program Counter
- **A** - A register
- **X** - X register
- **Y** - Y register
- **SP** - Stack Pointer (or S register)

Some other important values include:

- **V** - Current vertical position (scanline)
- **H** - Current horizontal position

```
PC F041 - - - - - V-39 H-62
 A 07
 X 00
 Y C0    SP FF

$80:  46 A8 34 8D E6 F2 01 FF 40 00 00 00 01 10 FF FF
$90:  FF FF FF FF FF FF FF FF FF EF FF FF FF FF FF FF
$A0:  FF FF FF FF FF FF FF FF FF FF FF FF FF FF FF FF
$B0:  FF FF 00 00 00 00 00 00 00 00 00 00 00 00 00 00
$C0:  00 00 00 00 00 00 00 00 00 00 00 00 00 00 00 00
$D0:  00 00 00 00 00 00 00 00 00 00 00 00 00 00 00 00
$E0:  00 00 00 00 00 00 00 00 00 00 00 00 00 00 00 00
$F0:  00 00 00 00 00 00 00 00 00 00 00 00 00 0F 7F F2
```

Figure 2.5: Debug Window

2.2 Keyboard Shortcuts

You can click on the Settings icon in the lower-right of the emulator window to display keyboard shortcuts. You usually have to click on the emulator before using them. There are a few that are particularly useful during development (Note: On Macs, Ctrl might be Option/Alt):

Ctrl-G: Displays the number of scanlines drawn in the current frame. This can vary between frames, and as we'll see in upcoming chapters, it's important to make this a stable value (around 262).

Ctrl-D: Toggles between debug modes, which displays different colors for various game objects.

Ctrl-C: Enable/disable collisions.

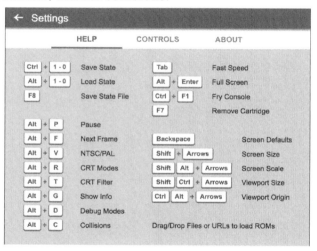

Figure 2.6: Emulator Keyboard Shortcuts

> **NOTE:** The IDE is under active development and may differ from what we describe here.

3

VCS Memory Map

One vital aspect of the VCS that we must cover is where things are located in address space. "Where" means at which addresses. Due to its 16-bit address bus, there are 65,536 (2^{16}) possible addresses that the 6502 can access. Most of those addresses are unused on the VCS.

There are three components connected to the VCS bus:

- TIA (Television Interface Adapter) - The main video and sound chip.
- PIA (Peripheral Interface Adapter) - RAM, timers, and controller input.
- ROM (Read Only Memory) - The 6502 program code included on the game cartridge.

Each component is responsible for handling read and write commands for a range of addresses. We organize these addresses into a *memory map* so that we can easily remember which addresses correspond to which component. Figure 3.1 provides an overview of this address space breakdown; a more detailed list is in Appendix A: VCS Memory Map.

3.1 Equates

No one likes keeping a bunch of weird numbers in their head, so the assembler helps you track all of these memory locations. You can define *equates*, which assign names to memory locations

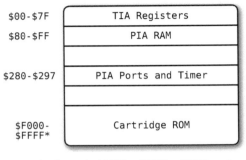

$00-$7F	TIA Registers
$80-$FF	PIA RAM
$280-$297	PIA Ports and Timer
$F000- $FFFF*	Cartridge ROM

* also at $1000, $3000, $5000, etc.

Figure 3.1: Memory Map

and other constants for programming convenience. Most of the TIA/PIA memory locations are already defined in the include file vcs.h. For example, it defines the COLUBK background color register, which maps to address $09:

```
COLUBK      ds 1    ; $09   xxxx xxx0   Color-Luminance
```

To use it, you just include the vcs.h file, which should be done in pretty much every VCS program you write. For example:

```
include "vcs.h"

org $f000
lda #$ff          ; pale yellow
sta COLUBK        ; change background color
```

We can also define our own equates. For example, if we wanted to define a variable LivesLeft at memory location $81 (in RAM), we'd just say:

```
LivesLeft        equ      $81
```

We could also define the number of starting lives as a constant:

```
StartLives       equ      5        ; start with five lives
```

Using an equate is easy: just type its name. You may be tempted to do something like this:

24

```
lda StartLives  ; load the number 5 (WRONG!!!!)
sta LivesLeft   ; store in memory
```

But this would load the value at address $5, not the number 5! So we add a "#" to let the assembler know that StartLives should be treated as a constant:

```
lda #StartLives ; load the number 5 with "#"
sta LivesLeft   ; store in memory
```

3.2 Segments

The assembler can separate definitions and instructions into *segments*, which is useful for declaring variables. Since the VCS's RAM starts at address $80, we declare an "uninitialized segment" with the SEG.U directive, and then declare some variables:

```
seg.u   Variables
org     $80

DataByte    .byte   ; declare 8-bit value
DataWord    .word   ; declare 16-bit value
DataArray   ds 20   ; reserve 20 bytes for array
```

The assembler will reserve one byte at $80 for the DataByte variable, one word (two bytes) at $81 for the DataWord variable, and 20 bytes for the DataArray variable starting at $83.

This is often more convenient and foolproof than separate EQU instructions, since the assembler ensures that variables do not overlap in memory. Sometimes, though, you want multiple labels to reference the same memory location – you can use EQU for that:

```
Temp1       .byte       ; declare byte
Temp2       equ Temp1   ; same as Temp1 address
```

Our "uninitialized" segment just reserves space, it doesn't let you generate code. When we're ready to write code, we'll declare an initialized segment called Code (the name isn't important). Then use the ORG directive to set the code's origin. This

25

tells the assembler that our code will start at a certain address. Our generated machine code is not *relocatable*, which means that it must be loaded at a certain address to work properly. For the VCS, that address starts at $f000:

```
seg Code
org $f000        ; start code at $f000
```

Note that because the VCS only has 13 address pins, and only recognizes 8,192 ($2000) unique addresses, you could actually declare the origin as $1000, $3000, $5000, etc. This is trivia at this point, but we'll revisit it later when we learn how to use multiple memory banks.

4

Writing Your First Assembly Code

We now know enough to write our first VCS ROM in 6502 assembler. It won't do very much at first – we'll just draw some lines on the screen, but it'll introduce some key concepts we'll use throughout the rest of the book.

Our first line declares to the assembler that we are writing code for a 6502. This line is actually optional in the Web IDE because we add it automatically, but we'll include it here for completeness:

```
processor 6502
```

Next, we'll include some header files. There are a few standard files commonly used in VCS programming: `vcs.h` provides names for all of the hardware addresses you'll need and `macro.h` defines a few *macros* – templates of commonly-used functions that can be included as needed.

```
include "vcs.h"
include "macro.h"
```

After listing our header files, we define our code segment:

```
seg Code
org $f000        ; start code at $f000
```

A typical thing to do on the VCS is to initialize several flags and registers when the cartridge starts or is reset. We also make sure the stack pointer starts at $FF which will give the stack as much room as possible if we use subroutines:

```
Start   sei             ; disable interrupts
        cld             ; disable BCD math mode
        ldx  #$ff       ; init stack pointer to $FF
        txs             ; transfer X register to S register
```

(Oddly, most Atari 2600 cartridges from back in the day have a SEI instruction at the beginning to disable interrupts even though the interrupt pin is not even exposed on the 6507 chip in the console. Maybe it's a fear of spurious voltages on the pin, or maybe just a superstition...who knows. Anyway, it's just one byte.)

Next, we want to make sure the memory and the hardware is reset to a known state, since in the "real world" (i.e. non-emulator), it will be more or less in a random state. The easy way to do this is to set the entire zero page region ($00-$FF) to zero, which includes the entire TIA register space and the entire RAM space:

```
        lda #0          ; set A register to zero
        ldx #$ff        ; set X to #$ff
ZeroZP  sta $0,X        ; store A register at address ($0 + X)
        dex             ; decrement X by one
        bne ZeroZP      ; branch until X is zero
```

(Note: We could have left out the LDX #$ff since previous instructions have already set X to that value.)

The TIA chip doesn't mind having all of its registers set to zero, and will respond by generating an utterly black screen. VCS programming is mainly about setting various TIA registers at the appropriate time. For instance, we'll tell it to make the background color red:

```
        lda #$30        ; load value into A ($30 is deep red)
        sta COLUBK      ; store A into the background color
    register
```

Normally, we'd do a lot more here, but since this is our first program, we'll make it short. We'll tell the CPU to return to the start (literally the label Start) and do everything all over again.

```
jmp Start
```

Finally, we'll use the ORG directive again so we can do two things: Fill out the ROM size to exactly 4K (4096 or $1000) bytes in size, and tell the 6502 where our program will start. When the 6502 is reset, it reads a 16-bit address from location $FFFC/$FFFD and sets the instruction pointer there. The .WORD directive will emit that two-byte address verbatim:

```
org $fffc
.word Start      ; reset vector at $fffc
.word Start      ; interrupt vector at $fffe (unused in
VCS)
```

The second Start vector is used for interrupts, which the VCS doesn't use, but we include it anyway so that our ROM is exactly the right size.

What do we see when we load this program? We should see alternating thick black and white horizontal lines. This is because we spent some time setting all of the TIA registers to zero, which made the output black, then we set the background color to red, then repeated the process forever. We never instructed the TIA to tell the TV where the frame begins! We'll correct this in the next chapter.

TIP: Use the VCS emulator at 8bitworkshop.com and the Hello 6502 and TIA example to review and modify the code discussed in this chapter.

Painting on the CRT

Our previous program generated some colors on the display, but not in a controlled way. We'll fix that now and explain some core concepts behind graphic generation on the VCS.

The VCS was designed to work in lockstep with a ubiquitous 1970s-era fixture, the CRT television. These TVs were designed to standards (NTSC in North America and PAL in Europe) that dictated certain timing constraints. These, in turn, will dictate our program's structure.

A cathode ray tube (CRT) has an electron beam that paints horizontal lines of pixels, or "scanlines" from left-to-right. The NTSC standard recommends 262.5 scanlines per frame, 60 frames per second. (We'll round that down to 262, because that extra half of a scanline relates to interlacing and isn't worth our time right now.) The TIA chip is responsible for generating scanlines, as described in the Stella Programmer's Guide[4]:

> When the electron beam scans across the TV screen and reaches the right edge, it must be turned off and moved back to the left edge of the screen to begin the next scan line. The TIA takes care of this automatically, independent of the microprocessor. A 3.58 MHz oscillator generates clock pulses called "color clocks" which go into a pulse counter in the TIA. This counter allows 160 color clocks for

the beam to reach the right edge, then generates a horizontal sync signal (HSYNC) to return the beam to the left edge. It also generates the signal to turn the beam off (horizontal blanking, or HBLANK) during its return time of 68 color clocks. Total round trip for the electron beam is 160 + 68 = 228 color clocks. Again, all the horizontal timing is taken care of by the TIA without assistance from the microprocessor. (Wright, 1979, Section 3.1)

A "color clock" is equivalent to a pixel. There are 160 visible color clocks, so the TIA outputs 160 visible pixels per scanline.

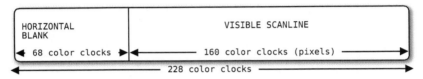

Figure 5.1: Anatomy of a Scanline

In a more modern computer, all of the pixels for a frame would be stored in memory. The VCS doesn't have nearly enough memory to store pixels for the entire frame, or even pixels for a single scanline – in 1977, enough RAM to store 160x192 full-color pixels would cost several thousand dollars. So it was designed so that the CPU could reprogram the TIA chip on a line-by-line basis.

The basic idea is that the CPU should change registers in the TIA during the horizontal blank period (the first 68 color clocks), perform some internal logic during the next 160 color clocks while the scanline is being drawn, and then wait for the next scanline to begin. Some people call this "racing the beam" because programs must always be aware of where the electron beam is at every step of the program. This is described in the Guide[4]:

The microprocessor's clock is the 3.58 MHz oscillator divided by 3, so one machine cycle is 3 color clocks. Therefore, one complete scan line of 228 color clocks allows only 76 machine cycles (228/3 = 76) per scan line. The microprocessor must be synchronized with the TIA on a line-by-line basis, but program loops and branches take unpredictable lengths of time. To solve this software sync. problem, the programmer can use the WSYNC (Wait for SYNC) strobe register. Simply writing to the WSYNC causes the microprocessor to halt until the electron beam reaches the right edge of the screen, then the microprocessor resumes operation at the beginning of the 68 color clocks for horizontal blanking. (Wright, 1979, Section 3.2)

You can think of WSYNC as a "skip to the next scanline" register. So a typical video routine looks like this (see Figure 5.2):

1. Strobe (write to) WSYNC to halt the CPU until the next scanline starts.
2. During the initial HBLANK period, write whatever TIA registers are needed to draw this scanline.
3. While the scanline is drawing, do any additional operations needed to prepare for the next scanline.

Since one CPU cycle = three TIA clocks, we only have 22 CPU cycles during the HBLANK period to safely set registers, and then 53 CPU cycles to prepare for the next scanline.

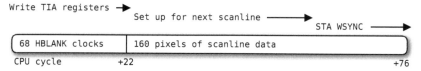

Figure 5.2: Setting up the TIA for a scanline

5.1 Timing is Everything

So we know we can program the TIA on each scanline to draw stuff and handle the horizontal timing. What about the vertical timing? Well, we have to do that ourselves. An "official" NTSC frame looks something like this:

33

- Three lines of VSYNC signal (dictated by the NTSC standard)
- 37 lines of vertical blank, or VBLANK
- 192 lines of visible scanlines
- 30 lines of overscan

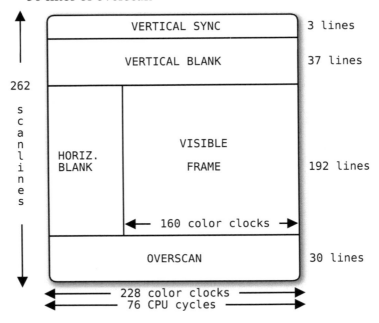

Figure 5.3: An official NTSC-compliant video frame

The 37 lines of VBLANK and 30 lines of overscan are periods when the electron beam is to be turned off; this was used to prevent the electron beam from being visible as it traced from the lower-right to the upper-left of the screen for the next frame. The TIA has a special bit that creates this "blacker than black" signal, but most emulators don't care if you set it or not.

The VBLANK and overscan also creates a safe margin on the top and bottom of the frame, since TVs were manufactured with differing numbers of visible lines. Most TVs will display some lines above and below the 192 visible lines recommended, and can even handle if the total number of lines is a few more or less than the recommended 262. It's important to be consistent, however, or the picture can "jump."

The three lines of VSYNC are essential, though, because they tell the TV that a frame has ended and a new frame is beginning.

Hex Addr	Name	Bits Used 76543210	Description
00	VSYNC	......x.	Vertical Sync
01	VBLANK	xx....x.	Vertical Blank
02	WSYNC	strobe	Wait for Horizontal Blank

Table 5.1: Frame and Scanline Sync Registers

5.2 Making Rainbows

Enough talk, let's make some rainbows! We start with the same preamble as last time:

```
    include "vcs.h"
    include "macro.h"
    org  $f000
```

We're also going to define a variable in memory at the address $81. This will hold a background color that we'll use later:

```
BGColor        equ $81
```

We're also going to use one of our predefined macros to save some typing. Macros are code "templates" that are expanded on-demand. You can define your own, but some are predefined in the above macro.h file.

This macro is called CLEAN_START. It initializes the CPU and zeros out memory just like in the previous chapter, but it uses fewer instructions and it's easier to type. Since it's at the beginning of our program, we'll give it the Start label:

```
Start
        CLEAN_START    ; macro to safely clear memory and TIA
```

Macros are expanded inside of your code and take up additional ROM space. They may also modify registers or flags – so be aware of this when using them.

Now we're ready to start outputting a frame! Because we'll visit this routine repeatedly, we'll also give it a label. The first thing we do is enable the VBLANK and VSYNC bits in the TIA:

```
NextFrame
        lda #2          ; same as binary #%00000010
        sta VBLANK      ; turn on VBLANK
        sta VSYNC       ; turn on VSYNC
```

Now that we're emitting a VSYNC signal, we need to hold it for three scanlines. We strobe this register (i.e., write to it) to make it halt the CPU until the next scanline begins. If we do this three times, the TIA will have generated our three lines of VSYNC signal and can then turn off the VSYNC bit:

```
        sta WSYNC       ; first scanline
        sta WSYNC       ; second scanline
        sta WSYNC       ; third scanline
        lda #0
        sta VSYNC       ; turn off VSYNC
```

WSYNC doesn't care which value is stored – it triggers the CPU to wait as soon as it receives any write command. A register that triggers an action like this is commonly called a *strobe* register.

We'll now let the TIA output the recommended 37 lines of VBLANK. The TIA's VBLANK bit is still set, so we'll just loop 37 times, hitting WSYNC each time. We use the X register to count down the number of scanlines:

```
        ldx #37         ; count 37 scanlines
LVBlank
        sta WSYNC       ; wait for next scanline
        dex             ; decrement X
        bne LVBlank     ; loop while X != 0
```

At this point, we're now ready to start drawing to the screen. Let's first disable VBLANK which releases the TIA to generate some color:

```
lda #0
sta VBLANK        ; turn off VBLANK
```

Next, we'll draw our 192 visible scanlines. We'll use X again to count. We'll also load Y with the BGColor variable before the loop, incrementing it each loop iteration. This will paint a different color for each scanline, creating a venetian blind rainbow effect:

```
        ldx #192          ; count 192 scanlines
        ldy BGColor       ; load the background color out of RAM
LVScan
        sty COLUBK        ; set the background color
        sta WSYNC         ; wait for next scanline
        iny               ; increment the background color
        dex               ; decrement X
        bne LVScan        ; loop while X != 0
```

After this, we'll output 30 more lines of VBLANK (overscan) to complete our frame:

```
        lda #2
        sta VBLANK        ; turn on VBLANK again
        ldx #30           ; count 30 scanlines
LVOver
        sta WSYNC         ; wait for next scanline
        dex               ; decrement X
        bne LVOver        ; loop while X != 0
```

For the next frame, we'll decrement the BGColor variable so that the colors animate down the screen.

```
        dec BGColor
        jmp NextFrame
```

We finish with the standard epilogue, as described in the previous chapter:

```
org $fffc
.word Start
.word Start
```

That's all we need to draw a NTSC-compatible frame. You can check our work by clicking the emulator window and hitting Ctrl-G – the display should read 262 lines.

6

Playfield Graphics

So far, we've managed to draw some colorful horizontal lines and learned how to output a proper NTSC-compatible frame for a television. Now we're going to draw some more complicated graphics.

The *playfield* is the lowest-resolution object that the TIA can draw. It was meant to be used to draw simple rectangular barriers, scoreboard digits, and other coarse objects. It's made up of 40 pixels which go all the way across the screen. Only 20 pixels are unique – the rightmost 20 are either exact duplicates or a mirrored reflection of the first 20, depending on bit 0 of the CTRLPF register.

We've learned about the COLUBK register, which describes the background color of the screen. There is also a COLUPF register for the foreground color of the playfield. The playfield bitmap is set in the PF0, PF1, and PF2 registers, which are arranged on the screen differently depending on the playfield mode in CTRLPF (see Figure 6.1).

Note that the four lower bits of PF0 are not used, and that the direction of the bits in PF1 are reversed with respect with PF0 and PF2.

Like everything else the TIA draws, the playfield has to be programmed line-by-line. If nothing changes, the TIA will just repeat what was on the previous line. You can change the colors

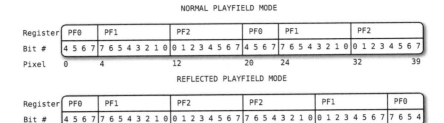

Figure 6.1: Layout of Playfield Register Pixels

and the playfield bits at the beginning of each line if you like (or during, but let's not discuss that now!).

```
        ldx #192        ; counts # of lines left
        lda #0          ; changes every scanline
        ldy counter     ; changes every frame
lvscan
        sta WSYNC       ; wait for next scanline
        sta PF0         ; set the PF0 playfield pattern
    register
        sta PF1         ; set the PF1 playfield pattern
    register
        sta PF2         ; set the PF2 playfield pattern
    register
        sta COLUBK      ; set the background color
        sty COLUPF      ; set the foreground color from Y
        clc
        adc #1          ; increment A
        dex
        bne lvscan
```

Here, we're just incrementing a counter and loading the value into each of the playfield registers. The result will look kind of like an arch (see Figure 6.2).

Note that we set all of the TIA registers immediately after the WSYNC strobe. We only have a limited number of cycles before the beam moves out of the HBLANK region and onto the visible part of the screen. This loop is relatively simple, but for some displays, it will be very challenging to set all of the registers we need to before the scanline begins drawing. Sometimes you

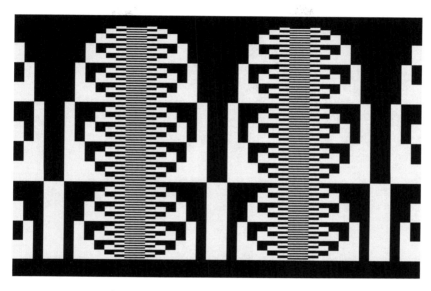

Figure 6.2: Example Symmetric Playfield

might hear such video display code called a *kernel*, denoting a small but well-optimized routine that is timing-sensitive.

To draw useful backdrops with the playfield, you'll typically have to set different register values for each scanline. Storing a unique bitmap for every scanline would require 192 * 3 = 576 bytes, so cartridges usually have some kind of simple compression scheme to reduce the playfield data to a managable size. We'll talk more about this in future chapters.

Hex Addr	Name	Bits Used 76543210	Description
08	COLUPF	xxxxxxx.	Color-Luminance Playfield/Ball
09	COLUBK	xxxxxxx.	Color-Luminance Background
0D	PF0	xxxx....	Playfield 0 (pixels 0-3)
0E	PF1	xxxxxxxx	Playfield 1 (pixels 4-11)
0F	PF2	xxxxxxxx	Playfield 2 (pixels 12-19)

Table 6.1: Playfield Registers

Coordinates

It's common on graphic displays to call the horizontal position the X coordinate, and the vertical position the Y coordinate. The X coordinate almost always goes left-to-right. The Y coordinate usually goes from top-to-bottom, but there will be times when it'll be more efficient to make Y go from bottom-to-top. Sometimes we'll even use both coordinate systems!

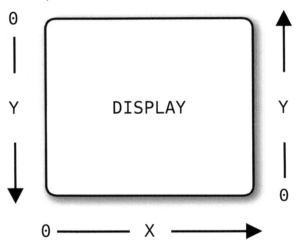

Figure 6.3: XY Coordinate Systems

We'll try to clarify which Y coordinate system we're using in the various examples. Also, we'll try to avoid confusion as to whether we're talking about X and Y coordinates or the 6502's unfortunately-named X and Y registers.

7

Players and Sprites

Now that we know how to draw the playfield, which usually serves as the background, let's draw some more detailed objects in the foreground.

The VCS predates *Pac-Man* and *Space Invaders*, and so it was designed with two particular 70s-era arcade games in mind: *Pong* and *Tank*. These were both games with very simple monochrome graphics and few moving objects. In *Pong*, a square ball is bounced between two rectangular paddles. In *Tank*, two rotating tanks fire at each other in a blocky playfield. The terminology for VCS's moveable objects – *players*, *missiles*, and *ball* – seem directly inspired by those games.

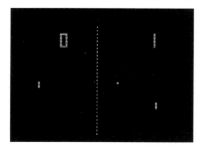 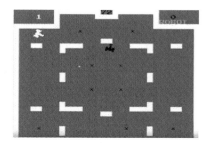

Figure 7.1: Pong and Tank

This chapter covers the moveable objects called *players*. The TIA supports two player objects, each eight pixels wide and one pixel high. They can be positioned anywhere horizontally on the scanline and the TIA remembers their position.

Hex Addr	Name	Bits Used 76543210	Description
06	COLUP0	xxxxxxx.	Color-Luminance Player/Missile 0
07	COLUP1	xxxxxxx.	Color-Luminance Player/Missile 1
10	RESP0	strobe	Reset Player 0
11	RESP1	strobe	Reset Player 1
1B	GRP0	xxxxxxxx	Graphics Bitmap Player 0
1C	GRP1	xxxxxxxx	Graphics Bitmap Player 1

Table 7.1: Player Registers

Note that we never said "sprites," since the term had not yet been invented! But you can draw sprites with the player objects by changing registers on successive scanlines, stacking up horizontal 8-pixel slices. Going forward, we're going to use *player objects* when discussing the TIA hardware, and *sprites* when discussing CPU routines that program the player registers on multiple scanlines.

The basic recipe for putting a player object on the screen:

1. Wait for the start of a scanline (do a WSYNC).
2. Set the player's bitmap register for the current scanline.
3. Set the player's color register (optional).

Like just about everything else in the TIA, the values you set persist across scanlines unless you change them. So if you don't need the player's color to vary line-by-line, you can set it before the frame starts. You must also set the player's bitmap to zero after the sprite has finished drawing, or you'll get a big smear of pixels going down the screen.

Here's a simple example of a sprite routine that pulls 16 bytes of data from an array named SpriteData in decreasing order:

```
        ldy #15             ; draw 16 lines of sprite
Loop    sta WSYNC           ; wait until next scanline
        lda SpriteData,y    ; look up sprite data
        sta GRP0            ; set player 0 bitmap register
        dey                 ; decrement Y
        bpl Loop            ; repeat until Y < 0
```

In this routine, the sprite begins drawing on the next scanline from wherever the TIA is currently drawing. It then goes through 16 scanlines before exiting the loop. At the start of each scanline, it sets the GRP0 register, which changes the bitmap for the player 0 object.

Note that all of our instructions take place in the HBLANK period at the beginning of each scanline. This guarantees that the player registers will be set by the time the TIA gets to the visible part of the scanline, no matter where the player is positioned horizontally.

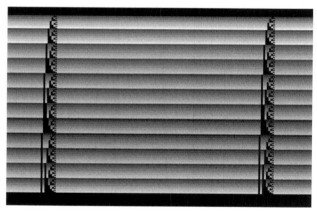

Figure 7.2: Players 0 and 1 over background

7.1 Horizontal Positioning

So far we've said nothing about setting the player's horizontal position! It turns out that this is a little tricky. It would have been nice if the TIA had an easy-to-use "Set Horizontal Position"

45

register, but the TIA designers went with a clever internal design that offloads this problem to us – the programmers.

To set the horizontal position of a player object, we have to wait for the TIA (and thus the TV's electron beam) to reach a certain horizontal position, then send a command to the TIA telling it to fix the player object to that position.

The TIA draws three pixels (color clocks) for every one CPU cycle, so we can build a loop and count the number of cycles for each instruction to figure out how many pixels have passed before we strobe the RESP0 register. The HBLANK period lasts 68 TIA clocks – so the CPU has to wait at least 22 CPU cycles for the TIA to start drawing the left edge of the screen, then wait until the TIA moves to the desired horizontal position.

Here's a quick recipe:

Assume X is the desired horizontal position of the sprite in pixels from the visible left side of the screen:

1. Wait for the start of a scanline (do a WSYNC).
2. Wait $(X + 68)/3$ CPU cycles.
3. Strobe (write to) the RESP0 register to fix player 0's position.

Some simple code might look something like this:

```
        ldx #5
        sta WSYNC       ; wait for scanline start
.loop
        dex
        bne .loop       ; loop 5 times, 5 CPU cycles each
        sta RESP0       ; fix player 0 horizontal position
```

Let's count both CPU cycles and the TIA clock as we execute each instruction:

Instruction	Cycles	CPU	TIA	X Coord.
sta WSYNC		0	0	-
dex	2	2	6	-
bne .loop	3	5	15	-
dex	2	7	21	-
bne .loop	3	10	30	-
dex	2	12	36	-
bne .loop	3	15	45	-
dex	2	17	51	-
bne .loop	3	20	60	-
dex	2	22	66	-
bne .loop	2	24	72	4
sta RESP0	3	27	81	13

Table 7.2: Example Timing of Horizontal Positioning Loop

Between the STA WSYNC and the end of the STA RESP0, we've used up 27 CPU cycles, or 81 TIA color clocks. So on the next scanline, the horizontal coordinate of the player will be (81 − 68) = 13 pixels from the left.

```
sta WSYNC
  dex
    bne .loop
      dex
        bne .loop
          dex
            bne .loop
              dex
                bne .loop
                  dex
                    bne .loop
                      sta RESP0
```

| HBLANK | X ← player position |

Figure 7.3: Instruction Timing of Setting Player Position

You might notice that the DEX/BNE loop takes 5 CPU cycles per iteration, which means 15 pixels will pass between each iteration. This means we can only position objects in 15-pixel increments using this method. This would lead to very jerky motion! The TIA designers accounted for this, and we'll learn how to do better in the next chapter.

8

Color Sprites

Now that we know that player objects can be used to create sprites on the VCS, and how to position them, let's draw some sprites!

Remember that we have to program the TIA on a line-by-line basis. It's the same for sprites. There are many ways to go about it depending on how detailed you want the sprite to be and how much CPU time you have in a given scanline.

Typically, games include a *lookup table* containing the bytes that define the on bits for each horizontal slice of the sprite. These go directly into the GRP0 register for each successive scanline.

Often, there will also be a *color table* containing the colors for each scanline. Sometimes this isn't used – especially in older games where it was common to have monochrome objects where the colors were set at the beginning of the game or before each frame.

When these tables map one table entry to one scanline, they are called "single-height" sprites. When a single table entry is used for two successive scanlines, they are deemed "double-height" sprites. Sometimes the bitmap table is single-height and the color table is double-height. You're writing the code, so it's your call!

The height of a sprite is only limited by ROM memory; it can take up an entire vertical screen column. It can be hard-coded or pulled from a lookup table.

Let's look at one example routine. We're going to hard-code the height of the sprite as a constant:

```
SpriteHeight    equ 17
```

Our sprite is really 16 scanlines high, but we're going to add one line for padding. The padding is a zero entry, and serves to clear the TIA register when we've finished drawing the sprite.

We also define a variable YPos, which holds the Y coordinate of the sprite:

```
YPos    .byte           ; Y coordinate
```

We have memory locations $80-$FF to play with (minus a few at the end if we use the stack), so we can choose anything within that range. In our program, this will hold the number of scanlines from the bottom of the visible screen (192nd scanline) to the bottom of the sprite – so we're using a bottom-to-top coordinate system in this routine.

Earlier in the program, we initialize this variable:

```
        lda #5
        sta YPos        ; YPos = 5
```

This places the sprite's feet five scanlines from the bottom.

Our routine begins right after the 37-line VBLANK period:

```
        ldx #192        ; X contains # scanlines remaining
```

First, we load X with the number of scanlines remaining, which we'll use to count downwards to zero. We could also start with zero and count upwards, but we save an instruction since we don't have to CMP to a number in the loop – we just repeat until DEX sets the zero flag.

In the first part of our loop, we subtract YPos from X to get a local coordinate relative to the sprite's position:

```
LVScan
```

```
txa                 ; transfer X to A
sec                 ; make sure carry is set
sbc YPos            ; subtract sprite Y coordinate
```

The SBC instruction subtracts its operand from the A register and puts the result back in A. Note that we set the Carry flag with SEC first – if it was addition, we would have cleared it with CLC.

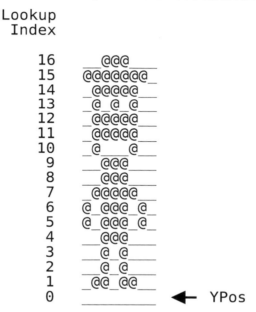

Figure 8.1: Bottom-to-top Sprite Layout

Now we have to see if this local coordinate is within the sprite bounds, meaning if it is less than zero or greater than the height of the sprite. It turns out we can do both by using the BCC instruction, which is an unsigned "less-than" comparison.

If the local coordinate is within the sprite's vertical bounds, we keep it as the index into the lookup table. Otherwise we set it to zero, which loads the blank padding entry:

```
cmp #SpriteHeight    ; are we inside sprite bounds?
bcc InSprite         ; if result < SpriteHeight, yes
lda #0               ; no, set index to blank entry
```

Now that we have our sprite index in the A register, we have to load the sprite bitmap data from the lookup table. The A register can't index, so we transfer it into Y to perform the lookup:

```
InSprite
        tay
        lda Frame0,y    ; load bitmap data
```

Next, we store it to the TIA register GRP0, which defines the pixels for player 0. We do a STA WSYNC first so that this happens in the initial HBLANK period of the scanline:

```
sta WSYNC    ; wait for next scanline
sta GRP0     ; set player 0 pixels
```

We can also look up a color entry for each line and set the player's COLUP0 register, which gives us a multicolored sprite:

```
lda ColorFrame0,y    ; load color data
sta COLUP0           ; set player 0 color
```

After this, we just decrement X and repeat the loop until we have completed the 192 scanlines:

```
dex            ; decrement X
bne LVScan     ; repeat next scanline until finished
```

The bitmap and color tables are included in the program ROM, usually with .BYTE or HEX directives. See Figure 8.2 for an example of a 9-line (including 0 padding) sprite with bitmap and color tables. These are defined in bottom-to-top order because that's the way the subtraction works out in the routine.

```
; Cat-head graphics data
Frame0
        .byte #0          ; zero padding, also clears register
        .byte #%00111100
        .byte #%01000010
        .byte #%11100111
        .byte #%11111111
        .byte #%10011001
        .byte #%01111110
        .byte #%11000011
        .byte #%10000001

; Cat-head color data
ColorFrame0
        .byte #0          ; unused (for now)
        .byte #$AE
        .byte #$AC
        .byte #$A8
        .byte #$AC
        .byte #$8E
        .byte #$8E
        .byte #$98
        .byte #$94
```

Figure 8.2: Sprite Bitmap and Color Table Example

You can create your own sprites with a nifty web-based tool, kirkjerk's PlayerPal[5].

9

Sprite Fine Positioning

We've figured out how to position player objects (sprites) horizontally to 15-pixel increments, but we'd like to do better than that. The TIA has fine-positioning registers that we can use to tweak the position of a moveable object several pixels to the left or to the right. We can set the "coarse" position using the timing technique in Chapter 7, and then set the "fine" adjustment immediately afterwards.

We can use the following basic recipe (example is for player 0):

1. Wait for a scanline to start (WSYNC).
2. Wait $(x + 68)/15$ CPU cycles and save the division remainder.
3. Using the remainder, compute the fine offset.
4. Write to the RESP0 register to fix the coarse position.
5. Write to the HMP0 register to set a fine adjustment from -7 to +8 pixels.
6. Wait for the next scanline (WSYNC).
7. Strobe the HMOVE register to apply the changes.

There are many variations on this routine, but we'll show you a common one here.

First, we wait for the scanline to start, and strobe HMCLR which resets any previous fine offsets that were pending:

```
lda #70      ; load the desired horizontal position
sec          ; set carry flag for SBC
sta WSYNC    ; wait for beginning of scanline
sta HMCLR    ; reset the old horizontal position
```

We've also loaded the desired X-coordinate (horizontal position) into the A register in preparation for our next step. We'd like zero to represent that the player will be flush left with the screen, and each successive value to be one more pixel to the right. (Those two STA instructions are strobes, so it doesn't matter which value gets stored.)

Next, we divide A (the X coordinate) by 15. Why 15? Because 15 is the number of TIA color cycles in our loop, as we'll see below.

The 6502 doesn't have a divide instruction, so we just subtract 15 until the result goes below zero. We'll use the SBC (SuBtract with Carry) instruction for this.

Note that we've set the Carry flag above in preparation for this step. The SBC instruction expects the Carry flag to be initially set, as opposed to the ADC (addition) instruction, which expects it to be clear. Also, when SBC wraps around below zero, it clears the Carry flag. So our loop will branch as long as the Carry flag is set.

```
DivideLoop
        sbc #15        ; subtract 15
        bcs DivideLoop ; branch while Carry still set
```

For each loop iteration, the SBC takes two CPU cycles, and the BCS (Branch if Carry Set) takes three CPU cycles (two on the final iteration). The TIA runs three times faster than the CPU, so it moves $(2 + 3) * 3 = 15$ color clocks (pixels) per loop iteration. We also subtract this number from the A register during each iteration.

As soon as A goes below zero, the loop ends and we're left with a remainder in the A register. We use this value to calculate a fine offset that will correct the player position:

```
; A now contains (the remainder - 15).
; We'll convert that into a fine adjustment, which has
; the range -7 to +8.
        eor #7          ; this calculates (23-A) % 16
        asl
        asl
        asl             ; HMOVE only uses the top 4 bits,
        asl             ; so shift left by 4
        sta HMP0        ; set fine position
```

That tricky calculation with EOR and ASL converts the remainder into a value appropriate for the horizontal motion register:

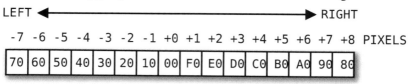

Value in HMxx Register (Hexadecimal)

Figure 9.1: Horizontal Motion Register Values

Now let's fix the coarse position of the player, which as you remember is solely based on timing. If you rearrange any of the previous instructions, position 0 may not line up exactly on the left side. (We'll show different versions of this loop in future chapters where this doesn't apply.)

```
        sta RESP0       ; reset coarse position
```

At this point, we've set the coarse position of the player, and we've set the fine offset in the HMP0 register. But the fine offset isn't applied until you do another WSYNC and then strobe the HMOVE register:

```
        sta WSYNC       ; wait for next scanline
        sta HMOVE       ; apply fine offsets
```

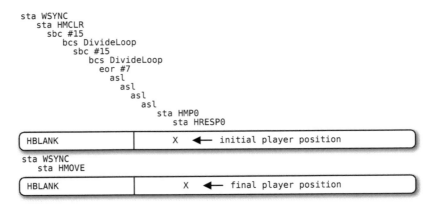

```
sta WSYNC
   sta HMCLR
     sbc #15
       bcs DivideLoop
         sbc #15
           bcs DivideLoop
             eor #7
               asl
                 asl
                   asl
                     asl
                       sta HMP0
                         sta HRESP0
```

Figure 9.2: Fine Horizontal Positioning with HMOVE

The HMOVE strobe must be right after the WSYNC or funny things happen.

There's no requirement that HMP0 be changed before RESP0, but we do it this way because the timing works out right. You can certainly rewrite this routine to suit different purposes – and we will, later on.

The HMOVE strobe applies fine offsets to all objects, so we could set the position of several moveable objects and then only do the STA WSYNC and STA HMOVE at the end of this process. It's common to do horizontal positioning in the off-screen VBLANK period since it usually takes the CPU's full attention for at least one scanline per object.

There are other ways to perform horizontal positioning besides the divide-by-15 trick – one early technique used by *Raiders of the Lost Ark* (and copied by several 3rd party carts) is to use a lookup table that stores the loop delay and the HMOVE register value in the same byte. But this uses a lot more ROM space.

Hex Addr	Name	Bits Used 76543210	Description
20	HMP0	xxxx....	Horizontal Motion Player 0
21	HMP1	xxxx....	Horizontal Motion Player 1
22	HMM0	xxxx....	Horizontal Motion Missile 0
23	HMM1	xxxx....	Horizontal Motion Missile 1
24	HMBL	xxxx....	Horizontal Motion Ball
2A	HMOVE	strobe	Apply Horizontal Motion (fine offsets)
2B	HMCLR	strobe	Clear Horizontal Motion Registers

Table 9.1: Horizontal Motion Registers

10

Player/Missile Graphics

Besides the two 8x1 sprites (*players*), the TIA has two *missiles* and one *ball*, which are just variable-length dots or dashes. They are similar to the player objects, except instead of an arbitrary 8-pixel bitmap, they are single dots that can be stretched to 1, 2, 4, or 8 pixels wide (using the NUSIZ0/NUSIZ1 registers, as we'll see in Chapter 17).

These objects share the colors of other objects. Missile 0 shares player 0's color, and missile 1 shares player 1's color. The ball shares the same colors as the playfield.

You set the horiziontal position exactly the same way you set the player objects using the RESM0/RESM1 and RESBL registers. But instead of setting a bitmap register, you just turn them on and off with the ENAM0/ENAM1 registers.

Missiles have one additional special ability – you can lock their horizontal position to that of their corresponding player by setting the 2nd bit of RESMP0/RESMP1. For example, you could set and then clear this bit whenever the fire button is pressed, so that a missile originates from the player's position.

Hex Addr	Name	Bits Used 76543210	Description
06	COLUP0	xxxxxxx.	Color-Luminance Player/Missile 0
07	COLUP1	xxxxxxx.	Color-Luminance Player/Missile 1
08	COLUPF	xxxxxxx.	Color-Luminance Playfield/Ball
12	RESM0	strobe	Reset Missile 0
13	RESM1	strobe	Reset Missile 1
14	RESBL	strobe	Reset Ball
1D	ENAM0	......x.	Enable Missile 0
1E	ENAM1	......x.	Enable Missile 1
1F	ENABL	......x.	Enable Ball
22	HMM0	xxxx....	Horizontal Motion Missile 0
23	HMM1	xxxx....	Horizontal Motion Missile 1
24	HMBL	xxxx....	Horizontal Motion Ball
28	RESMP0	......x.	Reset Missile 0 to Player 0
29	RESMP1	......x.	Reset Missile 1 to Player 1

Table 10.1: Registers for Missiles and Ball

11

The SetHorizPos Subroutine

We learned how to set the horizontal positions of movable objects in Chapter 9, but we'd like to make it easier. So we're going to introduce a subroutine called SetHorizPos that you can use again and again in your program.

As we discussed in Chapter 10, besides the two 8x1 sprites (*players*), the TIA has two *missiles* and one *ball*, which are just variable-length dots or dashes. They have similar positioning and display requirements, so we're going to make a subroutine that can set the horizontal position of any of them. But we can also use the HMxx/HMOVE registers directly to move the objects by small offsets without using this routine every time.

```
; SetHorizPos - Sets the horizontal position of an object.
; The A register contains the desired X-coordinate of the
    object.
; The X register contains the index of the desired object:
;
;   X=0: player 0
;   X=1: player 1
;   X=2: missile 0
;   X=3: missile 1
;   X=4: ball
;
SetHorizPos subroutine
        sta WSYNC          ; start a new line
        sec                ; set carry flag
.DivideLoop
        sbc #15            ; subtract 15
```

```
bcs .DivideLoop ; branch until negative
eor #7          ; calculate fine offset
asl
asl
asl
asl
sta HMP0,x      ; set fine offset
sta RESP0,x     ; fix coarse position
rts             ; return to caller
```

Note that the label .DivideLoop begins with a "." – this is called a *local label*. Local labels are only accessible within the subroutine. This ensures that label names don't collide across subroutines.

To use the subroutine:

1. Load the X register with the index from 0-4 of the object you wish to set (see comment section above).
2. Load the A register with the desired horizontal position.
3. Call the subroutine with JSR SetHorizPos.
4. Repeat steps 1-3 for other objects that need positioning.
5. To apply the fine offsets, do a STA WSYNC followed by STA HMOVE.

For example, to set the X-coordinate of player object 0 to 70, we'd do the following:

```
lda #70
ldx #0
jsr SetHorizPos
sta WSYNC
sta HMOVE
```

Also don't forget that HMOVE updates the position of *all* moveable objects, so you might need to strobe HMCLR or zero out any unwanted HMxx registers individually.

There are plenty of variations of this subroutine; for instance you could automatically do a WSYNC and HMOVE before the subroutine returns. But this would require two scanlines – for multiple objects, you could instead call SetHorizPos multiple times and then strobe WSYNC/HMOVE after you are done with all of them. There are also situations where cycles are so scarce you can't justify the JSR/RTS and have to inline or macro-include this code inside of another routine. This is part of the "fun" of VCS programming!

You will often call this routine in the underscan or overscan regions outside of the visible frame. One problem with this is that we should be counting our scanlines at all times, and these kind of complicated routines make it difficult to guarantee we'll get an exact number of scanlines. In the next chapter we'll discover another handy feature that makes this much easier.

You can also call SetHorizPos at the beginning of your program, and for the rest of your program just use the HMxx/HMOVE registers to move the sprites horizontally by small amounts. This is doable, but for most games it's just easier to call SetHorizPos on every frame for any moving objects.

12

The PIA Timer

One of the most challenging things about VCS programming is constantly tracking which scanline the TIA is drawing. The obvious solution is to simply count your STA WSYNCs for every routine and loop, making sure they add up to 262. This is acceptable for simple code, but what if you have some complex logic you want to execute? Scattering WSYNCs all over the place is awkward, and the resulting code can be difficult to analyze.

Never fear! The PIA (the 6532 chip that holds the RAM, as well as the controller inputs) has a timer circuit that comes to the rescue. Let's say we want to execute some logic during the VBLANK period before the visible frame starts. After the 3-line VSYNC we could set a timer that lasts almost for 37 scanlines. Then we do our time-intensive logic, and when finished we wait for the timer to fire. The TIA will happily output scanlines in the meantime, WSYNC or no.

There are four different timers on the PIA, each with different intervals. After a timer is set, it counts down to zero at the specified interval. For example, the 64-clock timer decrements once every 64 CPU cycles. This is the timer we'll use most often.

The basic recipe is:

1. Write a value between $01-$FF to one of the timer registers.
2. Do some computation.
3. Loop until INTIM reaches zero.

Hex Addr	Name	Bits Used 76543210	Description
0284	INTIM	xxxxxxxx	Timer Counter
0294	TIM1T	xxxxxxxx	Set 1 Cycle Timer
0295	TIM8T	xxxxxxxx	Set 8 Cycle Timer
0296	TIM64T	xxxxxxxx	Set 64 Cycle Timer
0297	T1024T	xxxxxxxx	Set 1024 Cycle Timer

Table 12.1: Timer Registers

To set up the timer, we store a value in TIM64T (for the 64-cycle timer). This is usually done right after a WSYNC so we know exactly how many scanlines we'll iterate through:

```
lda #nnn        ; load timer value
sta WSYNC       ; go to start of next scanline
sta TIM64T      ; store 64-cycle timer value
```

Then we go about our business, whether it's setting registers or just letting the TIA coast along drawing scanlines. When we're ready to wait for the timer to complete, we check the INTIM register. When it's zero, we exit the loop:

```
WaitForTimerDone
        lda INTIM               ; load timer value
        bne WaitForTimerDone    ; wait until == 0
```

We can't guarantee the timer ends exactly at the end of a scanline, only some time before it ends. You can add a STA WSYNC if you want to continue at the beginning of the next scanline.

Usually we want to wait for a given number of scanlines, which take 76 CPU cycles each. Each timer tick takes 64 CPU cycles, so how do we figure out which timer value to load to wait a given number of scanlines? We can leverage the awesome power of math to figure it out.

First, we need to figure out how many CPU cycles are used to set up the timer, and the worst-case number of cycles for the loop. The STA to the timer register takes four cycles, and the loop takes six cycles for each iteration. Add three cycles to make room for another STA WSYNC, and we have a total of 13 cycles.

So if N is the number of scanlines to skip, the target timer value is $\lfloor (N * 76 - 13)/64 \rfloor$.

We can also expose this functionality as macros and use them in multiple programs without doing the complicated math ourselves every time. In our distribution, these are included in xmacro.h. (See Appendix E for source code.)

To use these macros, just do something like this:

```
include "xmacro.h"

VERTICAL_SYNC    ; 1 + 3 lines of VSYNC
lda #2
sta VBLANK       ; turn on VBLANK
TIMER_SETUP 37   ; wait for 37 lines

; ... do some logic here

TIMER_WAIT
lda #0
sta WSYNC        ; wait for end of scanline
sta VBLANK       ; turn off VBLANK
```

The VERTICAL_SYNC macro generates 4 scanlines, the last 3 having VSYNC active.

Then the TIMER_SETUP macro performs a WSYNC and sets up the timer so that it fires 37 scanlines later. The corresponding TIMER_WAIT macro waits for the timer to count down to zero, and when it does performs another WSYNC so that we're at the start of the 37th scanline.

Using all of our macros described so far, we can create a minimal VCS program skeleton that outputs a proper 262-line NTSC frame (see Figure 12.1).

```
        processor 6502
        include "vcs.h"
        include "macro.h"
        include "xmacro.h"

        org   $f000
Start
        CLEAN_START
NextFrame
        ; 1 + 3 + 37 + 192 + 29 = 262 scanlines
        VERTICAL_SYNC    ; 1 VBLANK + 3 lines VSYNC
        TIMER_SETUP 37   ; 37 VBLANK
        TIMER_WAIT
        TIMER_SETUP 192 ; 192 visible scanlines
        TIMER_WAIT
        TIMER_SETUP 29   ; 29 VBLANK
        TIMER_WAIT
        jmp NextFrame

        org $fffc
        .word Start
        .word Start
```

Figure 12.1: Blank NTSC Frame Example

13

Joysticks and Switches

It's no fun to play a game without control! Fortunately, it's pretty easy to read the VCS's joysticks, paddles and various switches. In this chapter, we'll discuss how to handle data from input ports.

Hex Addr	Name	Bits Used 76543210	Description
3C	INPT4	x.......	Read Latched Input Port 4
3D	INPT5	x.......	Read Latched Input Port 5
0280	SWCHA	xxxxxxxx	Joysticks/Controllers
0282	SWCHB	xxxxxxxx	Console Switches

Table 13.1: Input Ports Registers

13.1 Console Switches

The VCS has a variety of switches on its front panel:

- A/B difficulty switch for each player
- Color/Black-and-white
- Game Select
- Game Reset

All of these are "soft" switches, meaning that the software program is responsible for their behavior, including the **Game Reset** switch.

Their values are read from address SWCHB ($282) and are defined as follows:

Bit #	Bitmask	Switch	Description
7	80	P1 Difficulty	0 = amateur (B), 1 = pro (A)
6	40	P0 Difficulty	0 = amateur (B), 1 = pro (A)
3	08	Color - B/W	0 = B/W, 1 = color
1	02	Game Select	0 = switch pressed
0	01	Game Reset	0 = switch pressed

Table 13.2: SWCHB Switches

The bit for a switch is zero when it's closed (depressed). A common way to read them is using the BIT instruction. For example, this reads the Game Select switch:

```
lda #$02        ; mask for bit 1
bit SWCHB       ; test bits
beq SwitchPressed  ; 0 = pressed
```

The BIT instruction performs the same operation as AND (logical-and of all bits) and sets the same flags, but does not store a result. You could have just as easily done this, using the bitmask:

```
lda #$02        ; mask for bit 1
and SWCHB       ; AND bits, result -> A
beq SwitchPressed  ; 0 = pressed
```

The BIT instruction has an extra trick, though. It sets the V (Overflow) and S (Sign) flags to match bits 6 and 7 respectively in the tested value. So if you wanted to test bit 6, the P0 difficulty switch, you might do this:

```
bit SWCHB       ; test bits
bvc AmateurMode ; overflow clear = 0 = amateur (B)
bvs ProMode     ; overflow set = 1 = pro (A)
```

This saves you one instruction and keeps you from having to modify the A register.

Many games only check the reset switch and, in fact, there's a shortcut you can use to do this. Just put the following in your main loop (assuming you're within 128 bytes of the Start routine, otherwise it's too far for a branch and you'll need a JMP):

```
lsr SWCHB      ; shift bit 0 -> Carry
bcc Start      ; Carry clear?
```

This reads the SWCHB byte and shifts it right, which moves bit 0 (the Game Reset bit) into the Carry bit. It'll also perform a write, but it'll be ignored. We then branch back to the Start label if the Carry bit is clear (which means the switch is depressed).

13.2 Joysticks

Joystick switches work the same way as the console switches. The directions are read from SWCHA and are mapped to bits as follows (0 = moved, 1 = not moved).

Bit #	Bitmask	Direction	Player
7	80	right	0
6	40	left	0
5	20	down	0
4	10	up	0
3	08	right	1
2	04	left	1
1	02	down	1
0	01	up	1

Table 13.3: SWCHA Switches

Here's an example of moving a value down and up by moving the player 0 joystick left and right. We can use the BIT instruction here, since left and right are bits 6 and 7:

```
        ldx XPos0
        bit SWCHA
        bvs .SkipMoveLeft      ; check bit 6 set
        dex
.SkipMoveLeft
        bit SWCHA
        bmi .SkipMoveRight     ; check bit 7 set
        inx
.SkipMoveRight
        stx XPos0
```

Buttons are mapped to bit 7 of INPT4 (player 0) and INPT5 (player 1), so you can check both of them with the BIT instruction:

```
        bit INPT4
        bmi .SkipButton0
        jsr Player0Button
.SkipButton0
        bit INPT5
        bmi .SkipButton1
        jsr Player1Button
.SkipButton1
```

There are other controllers on the VCS, like paddles and a 12-button keypad, but the joystick is by far the most popular, and it's pretty easy to support. We'll cover other controllers later.

14

Indirect Addressing

Up until now, we've used lookup tables like this:

```
lda SpriteData,y
```

This loads a value from the `SpriteData` address directly. But what if we wanted to choose between multiple sprites, or animate the sprite? We'd need a way to switch betweem different lookup tables.

14.1 Pointers

First, let's review addresses. We learned in Chapter 1 that they are 16-bit quantities, and take up two bytes of storage. We know we can use them as part of an instruction – for example, the `lda SpriteData,y` above. But we can also load them into RAM. These are called them *pointers*, and the 6502 uses them via *indirect* addressing modes.

We can declare pointers like this:

```
SpritePtr      .word   ; declare 16-bit pointer (2 bytes)
```

We can then load them with the address of our lookup table like this:

```
lda #<SpriteData
sta SpritePtr          ; store lo byte
lda #>SpriteData
sta SpritePtr+1        ; store hi byte
```

The #< and #> syntax tells the assembler to extract the low and high byte of the SpriteData address, respectively. (Remember when we talked about *little endian* – this means the low byte, or least significant, is first followed by the high byte.)

14.2   Indirect Indexed Addressing

We can use the pointer like this:

```
ldy #5
lda (SpritePtr),y      ; load value at SpritePtr+Y
sta Value
```

The expression (SpritePtr),y is an *indirect indexed* addressing mode. It means to look up the 16-bit value at SpritePtr and SpritePtr+1 (low byte and high byte), convert it to an address, then add the Y register to it.

If you know C, the following code is more-or-less equivalent:

```
static char* SpriteData = { ... };
char* SpritePtr = &SpriteData;
char Value = SpritePtr[5];
```

The indirect addressing modes only work in zero-page memory ($00-$FF) which happens to include all of the VCS's built-in RAM, so we're fine there.

14.3   Indexed Indirect Addressing

The other indirect mode is called *indexed indirect* where the
addition takes place before the lookup:

```
ldx #4
lda (SpritePtr,x)
```

Let's say that SpritePtr is at address $80. If X is 4, then we look
up the pointer at address $84, and then load the value contained
at the pointer's address. This allows us to declare arrays of
pointers in RAM. Since each pointer is two bytes, we'd have to
ensure that the X register is always even, or multiply the index
by 2 before using it:

```
lda #2   ; 3rd entry
asl      ;  * 2
tax      ; -> X
lda (ObjectType,x)
```

This mode is not as often-used as the (pointer),y mode in VCS
programming, because there is just not that much RAM for
multiple 16-bit pointers! Instead, many games use 8-bit offsets
like this:

```
ldy TableOffsets,x    ; lookup in RAM
lda SpriteTable,y     ; lookup in ROM
```

Instead of looking up an entire 16-bit pointer, we just look up
an 8-bit offset and use that to index into a ROM lookup table.
We are limited to 256 bytes, but that's enough for many VCS
programs.

In the next chapter, we'll use the (pointer),y mode to draw
sprites.

A Complex Scene, Part I

Now that we've learned about the playfield, player objects, and how to draw sprites, we can create a complex scene with a background and foreground. For this demo, the playfield will take up the entire screen, and we'll have a single sprite overlapping it.

This is a bit more difficult, because there are a lot of registers that need to potentially change during each scanline. To change the playfield, we need to set three different registers, and to draw the sprite, we'll need to set a bitmap register and a color register. We'll also need to look up all of this data in tables. This will make our kernel much more complex than previous examples.

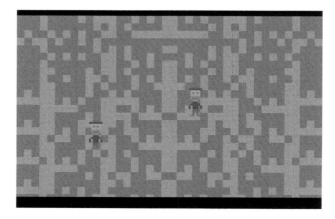

Figure 15.1: Two sprites over playfield

We'll achieve this using a *two-line kernel*, which means that each iteration of the main loop draws two scanlines instead of one. This gives us a little more wiggle room to move around loads and stores so that they happen at the right time. The tradeoff is that the playfield and sprites must align to even scanline numbers, but that's not a huge problem for many games.

To avoid confusing a single TIA scanline with a pair of scanlines, we'll call pairs of scanlines *2xlines*.

There are two parts to our loop. One sets up the playfield registers, and the other loads the sprite data. We don't want to store all 192 * 3 bytes of the playfield in memory, so we'll use a compressed storage format. We'll store the playfield in *segments*. Each segment is defined by a 2xline height and the three playfield registers. We'll only set the playfield registers when a new segment begins. In summary:

1. For the next playfield segment, fetch its height (in 2xlines) and playfield values.
2. WSYNC and store values to the playfield registers.
3. For each 2xline in this playfield segment, look up and set sprite bitmap and color data.
4. Go back to step 1 until we see a height 0 playfield segment.

The data defining the playfield looks something like this:

```
        align $100; make sure data doesn't cross page boundary
PlayfieldData
        .byte   4,#%00000000,#%11111110,#%00110000
        .byte   8,#%11000000,#%00000001,#%01001000
        .byte  15,#%00100000,#%01111110,#%10000100
        .byte  20,#%00010000,#%10000000,#%00010000
        .byte  20,#%00010000,#%01100011,#%10011000
        .byte  15,#%00100000,#%00001100,#%01000100
        .byte   8,#%11000000,#%00110000,#%00110010
        .byte   4,#%00000000,#%11000000,#%00001100
        .byte 0
```

Each playfield segment takes four bytes, starting with the height and then the PF0/PF1/PF2 register values. The ALIGN directive ensures that it starts on a page boundary (i.e. the low byte is

$00) because the 6502 adds an extra CPU cycle when an indexed lookup crosses a page boundary, and this could mess with our timing.

We'll use the (pointer),y addressing mode here, as discussed in Chapter 14. This allows us to switch between different playfields – useful if we want the player to walk between rooms, for example. We'll also use this mode to look up sprite data so that we can switch between sprite graphics.

We'll first load the PFPtr pointer with the address of our play-field table:

```
lda #<PlayfieldData
sta PFPtr              ; store lo byte
lda #>PlayfieldData
sta PFPtr+1            ; store hi byte
```

Our loop starts by loading the first segment:

```
NewPFSegment
        ldy PFIndex       ; load index into PF array
        lda (PFPtr),y     ; load length of next segment
        beq NoMoreSegs    ; == 0, we're done
        sta PFCount       ; save for later
        iny
        lda (PFPtr),y     ; load PF0
        tax               ; PF0 -> X
        iny
        lda (PFPtr),y     ; load PF1
        sta Temp          ; PF1 -> Temp
        iny
        lda (PFPtr),y     ; load PF2
        iny
        sty PFIndex
        tay               ; PF2 -> Y
```

To review, we've loaded the height of the playfield segment and stored it in PFCount. We've also loaded all three playfield bitmap bytes and stored them in registers and a temporary memory location. The next step is to do a WSYNC and quickly set all of the playfield registers before the scanline starts drawing:

```
        sta WSYNC
        stx PF0           ; X -> PF0
        lda Temp
        sta PF1           ; Temp -> PF1
        lda Bit2p0        ; player bitmap
        sta GRP0          ; Bit2p0 -> GRP0
        sty PF2           ; Y -> PF2
```

Note that we've also loaded the memory location Bit2p0 and stored that in GRP0, the player 0 bitmap register. That's because we just did a WSYNC, and the sprite data can potentially change on every individual scanline. We'll compute that value later in the part of the loop that loads the sprite data.

Now we move on to the sprite loop, loading X with the number of 2xlines in the current playfield segment. We then see if our current scanline intersects the sprite:

```
        ldx PFCount            ; load playfield length into X
KernelLoop
        lda #SpriteHeight      ; height in 2xlines
        inc YP0
        sbc YP0
        bcs DoDraw            ; inside bounds?
        lda #0               ; no, load the padding offset
    (0)
DoDraw
```

The important thing is that we've computed the distance in 2xlines from the bottom of our sprite, and we've put that value in A. Now we'll use that to look up the color for this 2xline, and move it into a temporary location:

```
        pha                   ; save original offset
        tay                   ; -> Y
        lda (ColorPtr),y      ; color for both lines
        sta Colp0             ; -> colp0
```

We need to save the sprite Y offset that we just computed, so we use PHA to push the A register onto the stack. We'll retrieve it later with PLA. (We could have just as well stored it into a temporary location.)

The color table defines colors for each 2xline, not for each scanline. But our bitmap table has two entries for each 2xline, so that each scanline has a unique bitmap value and thus higher resolution. So we look up both of them in the table:

```
pla                      ; retrieve original offset
asl                      ; offset * 2
tay                      ; -> Y
lda (SpritePtr),y        ; bitmap for first line
sta Bit2p0               ; -> bit2p0
iny
lda (SpritePtr),y        ; bitmap for second line
```

Here we've PLAed the original offset and multiplied it by 2 with ASL. This is because our bitmap table contains a unique value for each scanline, and we have to read both of them.

Now, we WSYNC and quickly set all the values for our first upcoming scanline:

```
sta WSYNC
sta GRP0        ; 1st line of sprite -> GRP0
lda Colp0
sta COLUP0      ; Colp0 -> COLUP0
```

If we've run out of 2xlines for this playfield segment, we immediately go back and fetch the next segment:

```
dex
beq NewPFSegment        ; fetch another playfield
segment
```

Otherwise, we do another WSYNC and set the bitmap value for the second line in the 2xline, then go back for the next pair:

```
sta WSYNC
lda Bit2p0
sta GRP0        ; 2nd line of sprite -> GRP0
jmp KernelLoop  ; repeat sprite-drawing loop
```

As you can see from the timing diagram in Figure 15.2, all of our register stores take place in the HBLANK period, and we use the visible scanline period to lookup values for future scanlines.

This guarantees no visual artifacts no matter where the sprite is positioned horizontally.

Figure 15.2: Timing of Double-Height Kernel With Playfield

Our kernel loop isn't 100% optimized, and there are certainly a couple of cycles to save here and there. But you can see the tradeoff in VCS programming – visual complexity vs. code complexity. Our kernel only draws the playfield and a single multicolor sprite. If we wanted to add a second sprite, missiles, or a ball, we'd have to do even more code gymnastics. The code to lookup the playfield registers takes almost an entire scanline, and we don't have time to do much else when this happens.

We could also make further tradeoffs, like have two monochrome sprites instead of a single color sprite, or lower-resolution sprites, or a simpler playfield. It all comes down to how much you can get done in 76 cycles per scanline. This example shows you that you can get a lot done if you spread your logic across multiple scanlines and choose tradeoffs that have minimal visual impact.

> **TIP:** To review and modify this code in the VCS emulator, visit 8bitworkshop.com and select the Playfield + Sprite I example.

16

A Complex Scene, Part II

In the last chapter, we drew a scene with a complex playfield and a single sprite. A game isn't very fun without at least one opponent, so we're going to write another kernel that supports two sprites.

Our previous kernel spent a lot of time loading the three playfield registers (PF0/PF1/PF2) and that limited what we could do on each scanline. This time, we're going to take a different approach. We're going to split our kernel up into four phases which draw two scanlines each:

1. Fetch value for PF0, update players
2. Fetch value for PF1, update players
3. Fetch value for PF2, update players
4. Store PF0/PF1/PF2, update players

Player register updates occur every other scanline, which reduces our effective sprite resolution. The playfield is updated every eight scanlines. This is similar to games like Atari's *Adventure* and *Superman*.

Our kernel will use a subroutine called DrawSprites to load the sprite data and write to player registers during each phase. The JSR/RTS instructions take an additional 12 cycles of overhead, so we can only really do this in a two-line kernel.

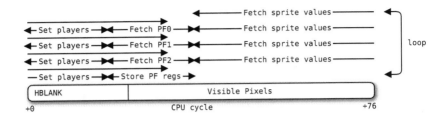

Figure 16.1: Timing of 4-Phase Double-Height Kernel

The kernel code would look like this:

```
KernelLoop
; Phase 0: Fetch PF0 byte
        jsr DrawSprites
        ldy PFOfs          ; no more playfield?
        beq NoMoreLines ; exit loop
        dey
        lda (PFPtr),y    ; load value for PF0
        sty PFOfs
        sta tmpPF0
; Phase 1: Fetch PF1 byte
        jsr DrawSprites
        ldy PFOfs
        dey
        lda (PFPtr),y    ; load value for PF1
        sty PFOfs
        sta tmpPF1
; Phase 2: Fetch PF2 byte
        jsr DrawSprites
        ldy PFOfs
        dey
        lda (PFPtr),y    ; load value for PF2
        sty PFOfs
        sta tmpPF2
; Phase 3: Write PF0/PF1/PF2 registers
        jsr DrawSprites
        lda tmpPF0
        sta PF0            ; store PF0
        lda tmpPF1
        sta PF1            ; store PF1
        lda tmpPF2
        sta PF2            ; store PF2
; Go to next scanline
        jmp KernelLoop
```

Our `DrawSprites` routine from the last chapter looks similar, except this time, we draw two sprites instead of one. Because timing is tight, we rely on one clever design feature of the TIA chip. If we set the `VDELP0` flag (see Table 16.1), we can write to the `GRP0` register for player 0, but the change won't take effect until we write to `GRP1`. (We'll explain this more in the next chapter.) This saves us from having to store and load a temporary value.

```
DrawSprites
; Fetch sprite 0 values
        lda #SpriteHeight       ; height in 2xlines
        sec
        isb yp0                 ; INC yp0, then SBC yp0
        bcs DoDraw0             ; inside bounds?
        lda #0                  ; no, load the padding offset
     (0)
DoDraw0
        tay                     ; -> Y
        lda (ColorPtr0),y       ; color for both lines
        sta colp0               ; -> colp0
        lda (SpritePtr0),y      ; bitmap for first line
        sta GRP0                ; -> [GRP0] (delayed due to
     VDELP0)
; Fetch sprite 1 values
        lda #SpriteHeight       ; height in 2xlines
        sec
        isb yp1                 ; INC yp0, then SBC yp0
        bcs DoDraw1             ; inside bounds?
        lda #0                  ; no, load the padding offset
     (0)
DoDraw1
        tay                     ; -> Y
        lda (ColorPtr1),y       ; color for both lines
        tax
        lda (SpritePtr1),y      ; bitmap for first line
        tay
; WSYNC and store sprite values
        lda colp0
        sta WSYNC
        sty GRP1                ; GRP0 is also updated due to
     VDELP0
        stx COLUP1
        sta COLUP0              ; store player colors
; Return to caller
        rts
```

Hex Addr	Name	Bits Used 76543210	Description
25	VDELP0	x	Vertical Delay Player 0
26	VDELP1	x	Vertical Delay Player 1
27	VDELBL	x	Vertical Delay Ball

Table 16.1: Vertical Delay Registers

We've also used an *illegal* instruction, ISB, which consists of a INC followed by a SBC. An *illegal* instruction just means that it's *undocumented*. We use it here to save a couple of cycles, because ISB is combination of two operations in a single instruction.

The critical timing happens after the WSYNC, where we write the registers for player objects. Thanks to the VDELP0 flag, we only have to perform three writes here. But in Phase 3, we write to the PF0/PF1/PF2 registers right after this subroutine returns. We've got just barely enough time left in the HBLANK period to write the first playfield register before the TIA starts drawing it. So we can't do much more after the WSYNC without affecting things downstream.

Before the WSYNC, we've actually got a lot of cycles left over (about 40 or so, depending on how many table lookups cross page boundaries) to do other things, like drawing missiles. But since our timing before the WSYNC isn't precise, we might update a register after the TIA has already drawn the object. This might be acceptable, depending on the game, because the missile will likely appear on the next line.

17

NUSIZ and Other Delights

There are a couple of other fun graphical features of the VCS provided by the Number Size (NUSIZ), Control Playfield (CTRLPF), and Reflect Players (REFP) registers that we should discuss here. Well, they're not so much *fun* as *convenient*, and it's worth taking the time to understand them. Table 17.1 lists each of these registers' hex addresses, names, used bits, and descriptions.

Hex Addr	Name	Bits Used 76543210	Description
04	NUSIZ0	..xx.xxx	Number-Size Player/Missile 0
05	NUSIZ1	..xx.xxx	Number-Size Player/Missile 1
0A	CTRLPF	..xx.xxx	Control Playfield, Ball
0B	REFP0	....x...	Reflect Player 0
0C	REFP1	....x...	Reflect Player 1

Table 17.1: NUSIZ, Control, Reflect Registers

17.1 Player Reflection

Let's say you have a little person that runs left and right. You'd like the sprite to face left when running left, and right when running right. Instead of having separate sprites for left/right, you can use the REFP0 and REFP1 reflection bits.

To display a mirror image of a sprite, set bit 3 (#$08) of the reflection register for the desired player object (REFP0 for player 0, REFP1 for player 1). Clear bit 3 to restore the original image.

17.2 NUSIZ and Multiple Player Copies

The NUSIZ (NUmber-SIZe) registers configure the size of player objects and also the number of copies. You can set it up to draw one or two additional copies of a player object on the same scanline, or to draw a 2x-wide or 4x-wide player. Games like *Combat* and *Space Invaders* take advantage of it to show formations of objects without much complexity.

Just set the lower 3 bits of the NUSIZ register for the desired player object (NUSIZ0 for player0, NUSIZ1 for player 1) according to one of these 8 configurations:

Figure 17.1: NUSIZ Number-Size Register Spacing

Multiple copies of missile objects are also drawn if selected in NUSIZ. These are selected with bits 4 and 5 according to the following table:

Binary	Hex	Description
00xxxx	$00	1 pixel wide
01xxxx	$10	2 pixels wide
10xxxx	$20	4 pixels wide
11xxxx	$30	8 pixels wide

Table 17.2: NUSIZ Missile Size Registers

You can set both player and missile values for a NUSIZ register by combining bits, for example setting NUSIZ0 to the hex value $25 sets missile 0 to 4 pixels wide (2) and player 0 to double-size (5).

17.3 VDELP: Vertical Delay

We've seen that sprite kernels can be very tight timing-wise. The TIA designers realized this and added a feature called *vertical delay* which especially helps with two-line kernels. We covered it briefly in Chapter 16, but we'll go into more detail here.

Internally, the TIA keeps two GRP registers for each player. For player 0, we'll call them GRP0(a) and GRP0(b). Every time there's a write to GRP1, GRP0(a) gets transferred into GRP0(b). The VDELP0 register selects whether the TIA uses GRP0(a) or GRP0(b) for outputting pixels. Similarly, there's a pair of GRP1(a) and GRP1(b) registers that are shifted whenever GRP0 is written.

In two-line kernels, the sprite registers are updated every two lines. This effectively halves your vertical sprite resolution, as well as your vertical positioning resolution. But the VDELP registers can give you full vertical positioning, if you alternate GRP0 and GRP1 writes on alternate scanlines. In this case, setting VDELP effectively delays the player's output by one scanline, so you can consider it a *fine vertical adjustment* of +1 scanline.

The VDELP registers also help when it's inconvenient or impossible to set a GRP register in the HBLANK period. For example, let's say we've set the VDELP0 bit. You can then set GRP0 in the visible portion of the scanline, and then when you set GRP1 in the HBLANK period, it'll trigger the output for GRP0 simultaneously.

The ball object also has a vertical delay bit (VDELBL) which works the same way for the ball enable (ENABL) bit. The missile registers, however, don't have any vertical delay feature.

17.4 CTRLPF and Object Priority

When objects overlap, the TIA assigns each object a priority and displays the object with the highest priority. The CTRLPF allows you to change these priorities so that you can have sprites that appear to overlap the playfield background, or vice-versa.

The normal priority assignments are as follows:

Priority	Objects
1	Player 0, missile 0
2	Player 1, missile 1
3	Ball, playfield

Table 17.3: Normal CTRLPF Priority Assignments

If bit 2 (#$04) of the CTRLPF register is set, the modified priority assignments are used so that the playfield and ball are in the foreground:

Priority	Objects
1	Ball, playfield
2	Player 0, missile 0
3	Player 1, missile 1

Table 17.4: CTRLPF Priority Assignments when Bit 2 is Set

17.5   Two-Player Score Mode

When bit 1 (#$2) of the CTRLPF register is set, the playfield is put into *score mode*. This makes the playfield take two distinct colors: it assumes player 0's color in COLUP0 for the left side, and player 1's color in COLUP1 for the right side. We'll use this feature in the next chapter to draw a scoreboard at the top of the screen.

Scoreboard

Displaying letters and numbers on the VCS requires the same do-it-yourself attitude as everything else. Early Atari games didn't have much except a simple numeric scoreboard, but soon cartridges like Warren Robinett's *BASIC Programming* pushed the 2600 to its limits by drawing full lines of text. In this chapter, we'll take a look at some common techniques for drawing text.

Figure 18.1: Example scoreboard

Letters and numbers on the VCS are usually represented by *bitmap fonts*. A common size is 4x5 pixels (the characters are actually 3x5, one column is always blank for spacing purposes).

A good strategy is to combine two 4-pixel copies of a character into a single byte, like this 9 digit:

```
.byte $EE ;  |XXX XXX |
.byte $AA ;  |X X X X |
.byte $EE ;  |XXX XXX |
.byte $22 ;  |  X   X |
.byte $EE ;  |XXX XXX |
```

This makes it easy for code to combine two digits into an eight-pixel-wide bitmap using the following procedure:

- Look up the most-significant digit's bitmap
- AND #$0F to extract the left digit
- Look up the least-significant digit's bitmap
- AND #$F0 to extract the right digit
- ORA the two values to combine the two bitmaps

Here we use a convenient feature of the 6502 called *BCD mode*. This allows numbers to be manipulated in a more human-readable format. Each four-bit half of the byte contains a decimal digit, so that the value expressed in hexadecimal reads the same as the decimal representation. For example, $00 to $09 are the same, but 10 is stored as $10, 11 is $11, etc. all the way up to $99.

The following routine takes a BCD-encoded number and looks up bitmap data for each digit separately, combining them into a 5-byte array in memory:

```
GetBCDBitmap subroutine
; First fetch the bytes for the 1st digit
        pha                 ; save original BCD number
        and #$0F            ; mask out the least significant digit
        sta Temp
        asl
        asl
        adc Temp            ; multiply by 5
        tay                 ; -> Y
        lda #5
        sta Temp            ; count down from 5
.loop1
        lda DigitsBitmap,y
        and #$0F            ; mask out leftmost digit
        sta FontBuf,x       ; store leftmost digit
        iny
        inx
        dec Temp
        bne .loop1
; Now do the 2nd digit
        pla                 ; restore original BCD number
        lsr
        lsr
        lsr
```

```
        lsr                 ; shift right by 4 (in BCD, divide by
    10)
        sta Temp
        asl
        asl
        adc Temp            ; multiply by 5
        tay                 ; -> Y
        dex
        dex
        dex
        dex
        dex                 ; subtract 5 from X (reset to original)
        lda #5
        sta Temp            ; count down from 5
.loop2
        lda DigitsBitmap,y
        and #$F0            ; mask out leftmost digit
        ora FontBuf,x       ; combine left and right digits
        sta FontBuf,x       ; store combined digits
        iny
        inx
        dec Temp
        bne .loop2
        rts
```

The previous routine does most of the heavy lifting, so our kernel is relatively simple. We draw the digits by loading the bitmaps of the scoreboard from memory, then writing the playfield registers twice – once for the left side, followed by a delay of several cycles, followed by a write for the right side:

```
        ldy #0              ; Y will contain the frame Y coordinate
.ScoreLoop
        sta WSYNC
        tya
        lsr                 ; divide Y by two for double-height
    lines
        tax                 ; -> X
        lda FontBuf+0,x
        sta PF1             ; set left score bitmap
        SLEEP 28            ; wait until TIA is done drawing
    leftmost digits
        lda FontBuf+5,x
        sta PF1             ; set right score bitmap
        iny
```

```
    cpy #10
    bcc .ScoreLoop  ; repeat for 10 scanlines (5 font
lines)
```

Note the SLEEP 28 before the second STA PF1 write to the playfield registers. We need to wait until the TIA has finished drawing the left side of the playfield before we reset the playfield registers. Our SLEEP gives us 28 extra cycles, so if we add up all of the cycle times of the instructions before the STA WSYNC, we'll write to PF1 on CPU cycle 48, which corresponds to TIA clock 48*3 = 144, which corresponds to visible pixel (144 − 68) = 76, right before the center of the display.

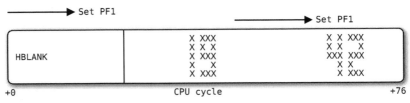

Figure 18.2: Scoreboard Display

You've got plenty of time to do other things in this loop, like change colors or even add additional digits (this would require more memory usage, however).

We forgot one thing: To first put the TIA into *score mode* which gives us two separate colors for the left and right half of the playfield:

```
    lda #%00000010  ; score mode
    sta CTRLPF      ; -> CTRLPF
    lda #$48
    sta COLUP0      ; set color for left
    lda #$a8
    sta COLUP1      ; set color for right
```

Collisions

Games need to know when objects collide. In the VCS, the TIA tells you when the pixels of any two objects overlap. This is one thing on the VCS that's actually easy!

The TIA has 15 different collision flags that can detect a pixel-perfect collision between any of the moveable objects – players, missiles, ball, and playfield. You can check these flags at any time – at the end of the frame is pretty common. When you're done checking (or before drawing the next frame) you clear them all at once by writing to CXCLR.

To see if two objects collided, just look up the register and bit index in Table 19.1. For example, to see if player 0 and player 1 collided, we'd look at the second row from the bottom, which has register CXPPMM and bit 7. The CX registers conveniently have all of their flags in bit 6 or bit 7, so we can use the BIT instruction:

```
    bit CXPPMM              ; player 0 - player 1
    bmi .PlayersCollided    ; bit 7 set? (bpl = clear)
```

To see if missile 0 and missile 1 collided (bottom row) we'd check bit 6 of the same register:

```
    bit CXPPMM              ; missile 0 - missile 1
    bvs .MissilesCollided   ; bit 6 set? (bvc = clear)
```

With the collision flags, we can easily test the player for collisions with the playfield and other objects. If we want the player

Register	Bit #	P0	P1	M0	M1	PF	BL
CXM0P	7		X	X			
CXM0P	6	X		X			
CXM1P	7	X			X		
CXM1P	6		X		X		
CXP0FB	7	X				X	
CXP0FB	6	X					X
CXP1FB	7		X			X	
CXP1FB	6		X				X
CXM0FB	7			X		X	
CXM0FB	6			X			X
CXM1FB	7				X	X	
CXM1FB	6				X		X
CXBLPF	7					X	X
CXPPMM	7	X	X				
CXPPMM	6			X	X		

Table 19.1: Collision Registers

to stop when they hit a playfield wall, we can just restore the previous position, like this:

```
; Did the player collide with the playfield?
        bit CXP0FB              ; player 0 - playfield
        bpl .NoCollision       ; bit 7 clear?
; Yes, load previous position
        lda YPosPrev
        sta YPos
        lda XPosPrev
        sta XPos
        jmp NoMoveJoy          ; don't move the player
.NoCollision
; No collision, update previous position and move player
        lda YPos
        sta YPosPrev
        lda XPos
        sta XPosPrev
        jsr MoveJoystick       ; move the player
.NoMoveJoy
```

20

Asynchronous Playfields: Bitmap

We learned in Chapter 6 that the playfield is made up of 20 pixels that are either repeated or mirrored on the right 20 pixels of the display. But this limits the kind of playfield you can draw, and often you want the right side to be distinct from the left side. This is called using an *asymmetric playfield*.

Remember that the playfield is defined by 20 bits in three registers - PF0, PF1, and PF2. Since we want 40 unique pixels, we need to program the TIA registers twice – once for the left side, and once for the right side.

We also need to time our register stores so that they take place after the TIA has finished displaying the previous value. If we do it right, we'll set two different values for each playfield register per scanline, and get 40 unique pixels per line.

We can draw full-screen bitmaps this way, although it takes quite a lot of ROM storage. We'll have one array for each playfield column, for a total of six arrays:

	Left Side			Right Side		
Register	PF0	PF1	PF2	PF0	PF1	PF2
Array Name	Data0	Data1	Data2	Data3	Data4	Data5

Table 20.1: Asynchronous Playfield Register Layout

Then, to draw the bitmap, we just iterate through the arrays (high-to-low is easier), copying each of the six array values to the PF0/PF1/PF2 registers. We introduce a little pause between the left and right sides:

```
ScanLoop
        sta WSYNC
        lda Data0,y
        sta PF0         ; store 1st playfield byte
        lda Data1,y
        sta PF1         ; store 2nd byte
        lda Data2,y
        sta PF2         ; store 3rd byte
        nop
        nop
        nop             ; 6-cycle pause
        lda Data3,y
        sta PF0         ; store 4th byte
        lda Data4,y
        sta PF1         ; store 5th byte
        lda Data5,y
        sta PF2         ; store 6th byte
        dey
        bne ScanLoop    ; repeat until all scanlines drawn
```

Our routine relies on precise timing so that we always set the second set of playfield registers after the previous playfield byte has finished drawing, but before the next playfield byte has started drawing.

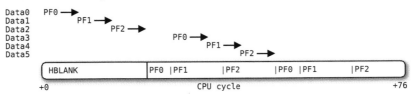

Figure 20.1: Timing of Asynchronous Playfield Kernel

For a full-screen bitmap, we'll need 192 bytes per array, for a total of 192 * 6 = 1152 bytes. Enough to render a blocky yet recognizable image of Ada Lovelace:

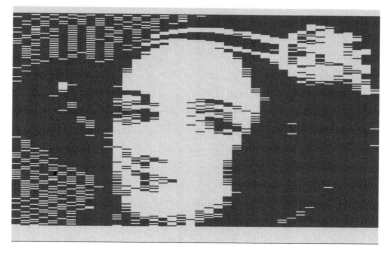

Figure 20.2: Playfield Bitmap of Ada Lovelace

One thing to be aware of is that the LDA aaaa,Y instruction takes an extra CPU cycle if the effective address crosses a page boundary. Pages are $100 (256) bytes long, so if we always align our arrays to page boundaries ($F100, $F200, etc.), we'll never cross a page boundary.

We can tell the assembler to start on a page boundary with the ALIGN directive, adding zero padding bytes until it hits a page boundary, but this wastes ROM space. For this example, we've left the arrays unaligned and made sure that even if we spend a few extra cycles, we'll always hit the acceptable range of CPU cycles.

As you can see, our bitmap doesn't look very good because the playfield has much more vertical resolution than horizontal. Later, we'll learn how to draw a smaller but higher-resolution bitmap using the player objects. (The *E.T.* cartridge used this technique to draw a smiling extraterrestrial on the title screen.)

21

Asynchronous Playfields: Bricks

We now know how to draw a playfield, sprites, missiles, ball, and a scoreboard. Now we're going to put them all together to make a rudimentary game!

We know how collisions work, so let's make a little *Breakout*-style game where the ball knocks out rows of bricks. We'll need to draw several rows of bricks, any or all of which might be missing.

We'll use the *asychronous playfield* technique that we learned in Chapter 20. Since playfield blocks will disappear as the ball strikes them, we'll have to store the playfield data in RAM. Our

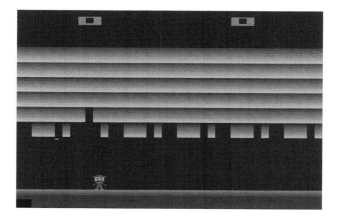

Figure 21.1: Brick game

array will have six bytes for each row of bricks – three playfield registers for the left side, and a different three for the right. If we have six rows of bricks, we have 6 * 6 = 36 bytes.

Register	PF0	PF1	PF2	PF0	PF1	PF2
Bit #	4 5 6 7	7 6 5 4 3 2 1 0	0 1 2 3 4 5 6 7	4 5 6 7	7 6 5 4 3 2 1 0	0 1 2 3 4 5 6 7
Array Index	0 1 2 3 4 5	6 7 8 9 10 11	12 13 14 15 16 17	18 19 20 21 22 23	24 25 26 27 28 29	30 31 32 33 34 35
Pixel	0 4	12	20 24	32	39	

Figure 21.2: Layout of Bricks Array

We've also got to track the X and Y positions of both the player and the ball.

```
Bricks          ds 36     ; brick bitmap (6x6 bytes)
XPlyr           byte      ; player x pos
YPlyr           byte      ; player y pos
XBall           byte      ; ball x pos
YBall           byte      ; ball y pos
```

In addition, we've got several constants that we use to make things easier when drawing the rows of bricks:

```
ScoreHeight     equ 20    ; height of top scoreboard
BrickYStart     equ 32    ; starting Y coordinate of bricks
BrickHeight     equ 16    ; height of each brick in pixels
NBrickRows      equ 6     ; number of lines of bricks
NBL             equ NBrickRows  ; abbreviation for number of
     brick rows
BytesPerRow     equ 6     ; number of bytes for each row of
     bricks
BricksPerRow    equ 40    ; number of bricks in each row
                          ; (two bytes have only 4 active pixels)
```

Our game will have several different kernels, each of which draws a different area of the screen. Because we draw the ball in all of them, we define a macro so that we don't have to duplicate code:

```
; Enable ball if it is on this scanline (in X register)
; Modifies A.
; Takes 13 cycles if ball is present, 12 if absent.
        MAC DRAW_BALL
        lda #%00000000
        cpx YBall
        bne .noball
        lda #%00000010   ; for ENAM0 the 2nd bit is enable
.noball
        sta ENABL        ; enable ball
        ENDM
```

The macro expects the current scanline to be in the X register, and then it enables or disables the ball if the ball's vertical position (YBall) is on the current scanline.

To draw the bricks, we have an outer loop and inner loop. The outer loop increments the Y register, which contains the current brick row index, and exits when we've drawn all the rows:

```
        ldy #$ff                 ; start with row = -1
ScanLoop3b
        iny                      ; go to next brick row
        lda #BrickHeight         ; for the outer loop, we count
        sta Temp                 ; 'brickheight' scan lines for
    each row
        cpy #NBrickRows          ; done drawing all brick rows?
        bcc ScanSkipSync         ; no, but don't have time to
    draw ball!
        jmp DoneBrickDraw        ; exit outer loop
ScanLoop3a
        DRAW_BALL        ; draw the ball on this line?
ScanSkipSync
```

The outer loop adds enough CPU cycles that we don't have time to draw the ball, so we skip drawing it when we transition to a new row. (We could have also drawn the ball but skipped the STA WSYNC, rearranging things so that the timing worked out either way.)

This is visually not very noticable, but since we're checking collision registers we have to be aware of a VCS maxim: If you don't draw it, it doesn't collide! Since the ball only disappears one out of every 16 scanlines, it's not a huge deal.

The inner loop looks pretty much like it did in Chapter 20, where we learned how to draw an asynchronous playfield:

```
        sta WSYNC
        stx COLUPF       ; change colors for bricks
; Load the first byte of bricks
; Bricks are stored in six contiguous arrays (row-major)
        lda Bricks+NBL*0,y
        sta PF0          ; store first playfield byte
; Store the next two bytes
        lda Bricks+NBL*1,y
        sta PF1
        lda Bricks+NBL*2,y
        sta PF2
        inx              ; good place for INX b/c of timing
        nop              ; yet more timing
        lda Bricks+NBL*3,y
        sta PF0
        lda Bricks+NBL*4,y
        sta PF1
        lda Bricks+NBL*5,y
        sta PF2
        dec Temp
        beq ScanLoop3b   ; all lines in current brick row done?
        bne ScanLoop3a   ; branch always taken
```

Each row of bricks is 16 lines, and since VCS color hues change every 16 values, we get a nice and inexpensive (in terms of CPU cycles) rainbow effect just by storing the current scanline into the COLUPF register.

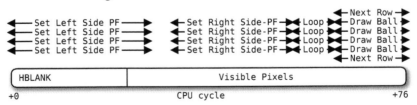

Figure 21.3: Timing of Brick Playfield and Ball Kernel

The player can never travel into the brick field, so our next kernel just draws the player's sprite and ball. It's conceptually similar to the routine in Chapter 8 except we also include the DRAW_BALL macro.

After we draw the frame and enter the overscan period, we check for collisions:

```
lda #%01000000
bit CXP0FB        ; collision between player 0 and ball?
bne PlayerCollision
lda #%10000000
bit CXBLPF        ; collision between playfield and ball?
bne PlayfieldCollision
beq NoCollision
```

First we'll talk about what happens when the ball is in contact with the player. When you press the joystick button, we set the Captured flag which allows you to grab the ball:

```
PlayerCollision
        lda INPT4                 ;read button input
        bmi ButtonNotPressed      ;skip if button not pressed
        inc Captured              ; set capture flag
        bne NoCollision
```

(There's a "bug" here because the Captured variable rolls over after 255 frames – but in VCS programming, we like to call them "features" and just get on with it.)

Now we see if the ball bounced off of the top of the player's head, or off of their shoes: We calculate $YPlyr+SpriteHeight/2-YBall$ to see if the ball is within the top half or bottom half of the player's sprite, and set YBallVel (the ball's Y velocity) to -1 or 1 accordingly:

```
ldx #1
lda YPlyr
clc
adc #SpriteHeight/2
sec
sbc YBall
bmi StoreVel      ; bottom half, bounce down (+1)
ldx #$ff          ; top half, bounce up (-1)
bne StoreVel
```

For the collision between playfield and ball, we need to check to see which brick we broke. This is pretty complex, so we separated it out into a subroutine. First, we correct the Y coordinate so that zero starts at the top of the brickfield:

```
; Subroutine to try to break a brick at a given X-Y coordinate.
; X contains the X coordinate.
; A contains the Y coordinate.
; On return, A = -1 if no brick was present,
; otherwise A = Y offset (0-brickheight-1) of brick hit.
BreakBrick
        sec
        sbc #BrickYStart          ; subtract top Y of brick field
```

Then, we divide by the brick height (16). We could have also done four LSRs, but this works for any BrickHeight value:

```
        ldy #$ff
DivideRowLoop
        iny
        sbc #BrickHeight
        bcs DivideRowLoop         ; loop until < 0
        cpy #NBrickRows
        bcs NoBrickFound          ; outside Y bounds of bricks
        clc
        adc #BrickHeight          ; undo subtraction to get
    remainder
        pha      ; save the remainder to return as result
```

We save the remainder to return as the result of this subroutine. Now, we compute $(X - 3)/4$ to get the brick column index (0-39) and use that to look up the array index (PFOfsTable) and bitmask (PFMaskTable):

```
        txa
        clc
        adc #3  ; adjust because SetHorizPos is off by a few
    pixels
        lsr
        lsr      ; divide X coordinate by 4
        tax      ; transfer brick column to X
        tya      ; load brick row # in A
        clc
        adc PFOfsTable,x          ; add byte offset
        tay                       ; array index -> Y
        lda PFMaskTable,x         ; bitmask -> A
```

We invert the mask with EOR (convert 1s to 0s and 0s to 1s) and AND it with the entry in the Bricks table. If nothing changed, we return a -1, otherwise we return the remainder computed earlier:

```
        eor #$ff                ; invert bits
        and Bricks,y            ; AND with brick table entry
        cmp Bricks,y            ; was there a change?
        beq NoBrickFound2       ; no, so return -1 as result
        sta Bricks,y
        pla                     ; return remainder as result
        rts
NoBrickFound2
        pla                 ; pull the remainder, but ignore it
NoBrickFound
        lda #$FF            ; return -1 as result
        rts
```

The subroutine depends on two tables that define the bitmask and byte offset for each of the 40 bricks in a row (the same layout described in 6:

```
; Playfield bitmasks for all 40 brick columns
PFMaskTable
    REPEAT 2       ; repeat twice
    .byte #$10,#$20,#$40,#$80
    .byte #$80,#$40,#$20,#$10,#$08,#$04,#$02,#$01
    .byte #$01,#$02,#$04,#$08,#$10,#$20,#$40,#$80
    REPEND                      ; end of repeat block

; Brick array byte offsets for all 40 brick columns
PFOfsTable
    .byte NBL*0,NBL*0,NBL*0,NBL*0
    .byte NBL*1,NBL*1,NBL*1,NBL*1,  NBL*1,NBL*1,NBL*1,NBL*1
    .byte NBL*2,NBL*2,NBL*2,NBL*2,  NBL*2,NBL*2,NBL*2,NBL*2
    .byte NBL*3,NBL*3,NBL*3,NBL*3
    .byte NBL*4,NBL*4,NBL*4,NBL*4,  NBL*4,NBL*4,NBL*4,NBL*4
    .byte NBL*5,NBL*5,NBL*5,NBL*5,  NBL*5,NBL*5,NBL*5,NBL*5
```

We call the subroutine like so, using the remainder value returned in A to see if we hit the top or bottom of the brick, and thus decide which direction to bounce:

```
PlayfieldCollision
        lda YBall
        ldx XBall
        jsr BreakBrick
        bmi CollisionNoBrick    ; return -1 = no brick found
; Did we hit the top or the bottom of a brick?
; If top, bounce up, otherwise down.
        ldx #$ff                ; ball velocity = up
        cmp #BrickHeight/2      ; top half of brick?
        bcc BounceBallUp        ; yofs < brickheight/2
        ldx #1                  ; ball velocity = down
BounceBallUpw
        stx YBallVel
```

We could have saved a little bit of work by checking the collision register after each row of bricks, so at least we'd know which row was contacted. However, this would require a few extra CPU cycles in our kernel that we don't have to spare (unless we wanted blank scanlines between brick rows).

The ball will constantly be in motion, so we need to track its velocity. We've got a signed value that tracks the Y velocity – it'll be either +1 or -1 (#$FF in signed representation). XBallVel is a fractional value; it's added to XBallErr every frame and the ball is only moved when the addition wraps the byte, so the ball can have speeds in the X direction that are less than 1 pixel/frame.

```
YBallVel        byte    ; ball Y velocity (signed)
XBallVel        byte    ; ball X velocity (signed)
XBallErr        byte    ; ball X fractional error
```

To move the ball horizontally each frame, we use the following routine:

```
        lda XBallVel    ; signed X velocity
        bmi BallMoveLeft ; < 0? move left
        clc
        adc XBallErr
        sta XBallErr    ; XBallErr += XBallVel
```

```
bcc DoneMovement ; no wrap around? no move
inc XBall       ; XBall += 1
lda XBall
cmp #160        ; moved off right side?
bcc DoneMovement ; no, done
lda #0
sta XBall       ; wrap around to left
beq DoneMovement ; always taken
```

The addition (ADC) sets the carry flag when it wraps, so the higher the XBallVel value, the more often this happens, and the more often we INC the ball position.

There's a similar routine for moving the ball left, with one important difference. In this case, the velocity is negative, and if you remember two's complement from Chapter 1, the byte value will be 128 or greater – so a signed value of -1 is the byte 255, for example. The lower our velocity, the *more* often we wrap the XBallErr addition. So we want to move the ball only when the carry from the ADC is clear (no wrap), not when it's set:

```
adc XBallErr
sta XBallErr    ; XBallErr += XBallVel
bcs DoneMovement ; did wrap around? no move
```

We'll learn another technique for fractional movement in Chapter 31 called fixed-point math that doesn't require a separate branch.

There are other tidbits here and there, like making a sound when the ball bounces, but feel free to study the source code and experiment using the Playfield + Sprite II example on the VCS emulator at 8bitworkshop.com!

A Big (48 pixel) Sprite

We've seen that the VCS graphics are pretty limited. During each scanline, we can draw 20 unique playfield pixels, two 8-bit sprites, and up to three ball/missile objects. We've seen in Chapter 21 how to draw 40 unique playfield pixels with some complicated gymnastics.

We've also seen that we can get six sprites on a scanline by using the NUSIZ registers, which draw up to three duplicate sprites per player object at configurable intervals. This is used in *Combat* for the three-airplanes-in-formation game mode, for example. But this still only gives us two unique sprites per scanline, and four clones.

We'll use a technique similar to the Asynchronous Playfields trick – reprogramming the TIA registers on-the-fly, writing to each register multiple times during the scanline. If we time our writes carefully, we'll be able to draw six unique sprites per

Figure 22.1: 48-pixel sprite

scanline, for example to draw a six-digit scoreboard, or one large 48-pixel sprite.

The first step is to set the NUSIZ registers for "three copies, close" to display three copies of each 8-pixel sprite, 8 pixels apart from one another. Our goal is to set each player's horizontal position so that they overlap like so:

```
Player 0       00000000        22222222         44444444
Player 1            11111111        33333333         55555555
```

Figure 22.2: Overlapping Players' Horizontal Position

The next step is to enable the VDELPx registers for both players. As described in Chapter 17, the VDELPx bit enables a buffer for the GRP register, so that when you set the player's bitmap register it does not take effect until you set the other player's bitmap register. This will be essential for our 48-pixel kernel, because it means we can pre-stage two GRP register values in the TIA chip, flipping them during the very tight set of instructions that sets the player registers.

Before the frame starts, we must also position the two player objects. They must be at an exact horizontal location, and player 1 must be exactly 8 pixels to the right of player 0 so that they meet with no overlaps. This does the trick:

```
sta WSYNC
SLEEP 20            ; skip 60 pixels
sta RESP0           ; position player 0 @ 69
sta RESP1           ; ...and player 1 @ 78
lda #$10
sta HMP1            ; player 1 goes 1 pixel to the left
sta WSYNC
sta HMOVE           ; apply HMOVE
sta HMCLR
```

So here's how we start our 48-pixel kernel:

```
TIMER_SETUP 192
SLEEP 40            ; start near end of scanline
```

We are going to be lazy and use the TIMER_SETUP macro to make sure we output 192 scanlines, even though our sprite is much

smaller. That macro also does a WSYNC, so we'll SLEEP 40 so that
we start the loop near the end of the scanline.

Now the loop. We start by loading the first two sprite bytes into
GRP0 and GRP1:

```
BigLoop
        ldy loopcount       ; counts backwards
        lda Data0,y         ; load B0 (1st sprite byte)
        sta GRP0            ; B0 -> [GRP0]
        lda Data1,y         ; load B1 -> A
        sta GRP1            ; B1 -> [GRP1], B0 -> GRP0
```

Because we've set the VDELP0 and VDELP1 bits, the first sprite byte
(B0) goes into the GRP0 buffer, not the real GRP0 register. This is
indicated by the [GRP0] notation.

The next sprite byte (B1) goes into [GRP1]. Since there is something in [GRP0], this triggers [GRP0] to store into the real register
GRP0.

```
        sta WSYNC          ; sync to next scanline
        lda Data2,y         ; load B2 -> A
        sta GRP0            ; B2 -> [GRP0], B1 -> GRP1
```

Now we've loaded the third byte B2, and that goes into GRP0.
Since we just stored B1 to [GRP1], that goes into the real GRP1.

Now we have to get ready for the time-critical step, the "one
weird trick." We load B4, B3, and B5 into the X, A, and Y registers,
with the help of a temporary location:

```
        lda Data5,y         ; load B5 -> A
        sta temp           ; B5 -> temp
        ldx Data4,y         ; load B4 -> X
        lda Data3,y         ; load B3 -> A
        ldy temp           ; load B5 -> Y
```

Everything's all set for the Grand Finale. We alternately store to
the GRP0/GRP1 registers four times with an amazing flourish!

```
        sta GRP1           ; B3 -> [GRP1]; B2 -> GRP0
        stx GRP0           ; B4 -> [GRP0]; B3 -> GRP1
```

```
        sty GRP1        ; B5 -> [GRP1]; B4 -> GRP0
        sta GRP0        ; __ -> [GRP0]; B5 -> GRP1
```

Since we have stored B2 in [GRP0] previously, these four writes store B2, B3, B4, and B5 to their appropriate registers in quick succession. Each instruction takes 3 cycles, which is nine TIA pixels. If we time it right, the writes will occur right before the TIA draws each of the four copies of the two player objects. Since we set "three copies close" in the NUSIZ registers, each copy of a given player object will be separated by eight pixels – about two CPU clocks of wiggle room.

The timing diagram looks sort of like this:

```
Player 0        00000000      22222222        44444444
Player 1            11111111      33333333        55555555
TIA clock  ................................................
CPU clock  .   .   .   .   .   .   .   .   .   .   .   .
    GRP0  B0          B2              B4
    GRP1  B1              B3              B5
```

Figure 22.3: Timing Diagram for Overlapping Players

Note that we really need the buffered registers that the VDELPx flags give us, because we only have three registers and simply don't have time to load a fourth register from memory in this sequence!

Note also that the final STA GRP0 is only there to ensure that [GRP1] gets moved into the real GRP1 register; the value being stored is irrelevant.

Now we decrement our counter and go back for another pass.

```
        dec loopcount    ; go to next line
        bpl BigLoop      ; repeat until < 0
```

There are plenty of other ways to write this loop. It's common to use the LDA (ptr),y addressing mode so that you can configure each 8-pixel column to point to a different bitmap – good for doing 6-digit scoreboards, "lives left" displays, etc. The crux of the biscuit is that 4-instruction store firing at the right time.

Tiny Text

Now that we know how to draw extra-wide sprites, we can apply this technique to another type of object: text.

We saw in Chapter 18 that we can draw scoreboards and other kinds of text using the playfield registers. However, these are pretty blocky, and limited to 40 pixels in width. Using the same technique as in Chapter 22, we can draw lines of text that are 48 pixels width by five pixels high.

Figure 23.1: Tiny text

The 48-pixel kernel is the same as before, but instead of fetching font data from ROM, we build a bitmap in RAM using lookup tables. Building the bitmap array efficiently is a challenge, because we've got to look up 60 bytes in memory and combine those into 30 bytes. If we did this without regard to performance, it might consume a few thousand CPU cycles, which would require 30 or 40 scanlines just to set up the sprite. Good luck writing very many lines of text!

Just like the scoreboard in Chapter 18, our characters are four pixels across (three pixels active) with two characters side-by-side in a byte, five bytes high (see Figure 23.2).

To use the routine, we'll first define a string of text:

117

```
         76543210
    0    .@..@@@.
    1    @.@.@.@.
    2    @@@.@@..        ◄── the characters A & B
    3    @.@.@.@.
    4    @.@.@@@.
```

Figure 23.2: Example 48-pixel font data

```
String0 dc "HELLO[WORLD?"
```

Our current routine is hard-coded to exactly 12 characters, but you could also make your routine recognize zero-terminated strings. Also, we've only got room for 50 characters in the 255-byte array, so we've had to rearrange some of them, which is why you see [instead of a space.

To build the sprite, we first set up a pointer to our string and JSR to the subroutine:

```
        lda #<String0
        sta StrPtr
        lda #>String0
        sta StrPtr+1
        jsr BuildText
```

BuildText uses a special trick involving the stack pointer (S) which we'll explain soon. First we'll save S since we'll be modifying it later:

```
BuildText subroutine
        tsx
        stx TempSP
```

We've got two variables that keep track of our progress, WriteOfs and StrLen. WriteOfs points to the end of the column of bytes being written to, and StrLen contains the current character being read:

```
        lda #FontBuf+4   ; +4 because PHA goes in decreasing
    order
        sta WriteOfs     ; offset into dest. array FontBuf
        ldy #0
        sty StrLen       ; start at first character
```

We process the characters in pairs, since two characters are packed into each byte column:

```
.CharLoop
; Get first character
        lda (StrPtr),y  ; load next character
        sec
        sbc #LoChar     ; subtract 32 (1st char is Space)
        sta Temp
        asl
        asl
        adc Temp        ; multiply by 5
        tax             ; first character offset -> X
; Get second character
        iny
        lda (StrPtr),y  ; load next character
        sec
        sbc #LoChar     ; subtract 32 (1st char is Space)
        sta Temp
        asl
        asl
        adc Temp        ; multiply by 5
        iny
        sty StrLen      ; StrLen += 2
        tay             ; second character offset -> Y
```

At this point, we've got the X register pointing to the offset of the first character's bitmap data, and Y pointing to the second character's bitmap data. All we need to do is look up both of these bitmaps, combine the two 4-bit nibbles into a single byte, then store the result.

If we didn't care about performance, we'd use a single table to look up all of the character bitmaps, and shift one by four bits to get them both side-by-side. But since we want to be time-efficient, we'll use two tables – one for the left nibble, and one for the right. They're the same, except one is shifted by four bits to the left.

There's also one more problem: We're out of registers! We've got to look up one table using an index register, then look up another table using another index register, use A to hold the combined data, then store it into a entirely different location

119

using a fourth register. We only have A, X, and Y, so it seems we're short a register. But we also have another register, S, i.e. the stack pointer.

What we'll do is set up the stack pointer so that it points to the end of the destination array, WriteOfs:

```
txa              ; preserve old X
ldx WriteOfs     ; load X with offset
txs              ; X -> stack pointer
tax              ; restore old X
```

The TXS operation transfers the X register to S, the stack pointer. (Only X can interact with S.) This means that whenever we do a PHA, we'll store A to the location S points to, then S will decrement by one. This allows us to quickly write successive bytes to memory, in decreasing order:

```
lda FontTableLo+4,y
ora FontTableHi+4,x
pha
lda FontTableLo+3,y
ora FontTableHi+3,x
pha
lda FontTableLo+2,y
ora FontTableHi+2,x
pha
lda FontTableLo+1,y
ora FontTableHi+1,x
pha
lda FontTableLo+0,y
ora FontTableHi+0,x
pha
```

That's all there is to it! Now we add five to WriteOfs to target the next column of bytes, and repeat until we run out of characters:

```
        lda WriteOfs
        clc
        adc #5
        sta WriteOfs
.NoIncOfs
        ldy StrLen
        cpy #12
```

```
        bne .CharLoop
```

After we've finished building the bitmap, we restore the value of the stack pointer that we saved at the start of the routine:

```
        ldx TempSP
        txs
        rts
```

If you wanted to save 256 bytes of space, you could use just one font table and do something like this:

```
        lda FontTableLo+4,x
        asl
        asl
        asl
        asl
        ora FontTableLo+4,y
        pha
        ...
```

However, this would add a few scanlines of spacing between lines of text due to the additional 240 CPU cycles required.

Drawing the sprite is pretty much the same as in Chapter 22, except we grab bytes from FontBuf instead of ROM:

```
        lda #4
        sta LoopCount
BigLoop
        ldy LoopCount    ; counts backwards
        lda FontBuf+0,y ; load B0 (1st sprite byte)
        sta GRP0         ; B0 -> [GRP0]
        lda FontBuf+5,y ; load B1 -> A
        sta GRP1         ; B1 -> [GRP1], B0 -> GRP0
        sta WSYNC        ; sync to next scanline
        lda FontBuf+10,y      ; load B2 -> A
        sta GRP0         ; B2 -> [GRP0], B1 -> GRP1
        lda FontBuf+25,y      ; load B5 -> A
        sta Temp         ; B5 -> temp
        ldx FontBuf+20,y      ; load B4 -> X
        lda FontBuf+15,y      ; load B3 -> A
        ldy Temp         ; load B5 -> Y
        sta GRP1         ; B3 -> [GRP1]; B2 -> GRP0
```

```
stx GRP0        ; B4 -> [GRP0]; B3 -> GRP1
sty GRP1        ; B5 -> [GRP1]; B4 -> GRP0
sta GRP0        ; ?? -> [GRP0]; B5 -> GRP1
dec LoopCount   ; go to next line
bpl BigLoop     ; repeat until < 0
```

Six-Digit Scoreboard

We can use the 48-pixel sprite methods in Chapters 22 and 23 to draw a six-digit scoreboard where each digit is eight pixels wide.

Figure 24.1: Six-digit scoreboard example

We represent the scoreboard as a BCD-encoded number, as seen in Chapter 18. Our score has six digits, which means it needs three BCD bytes. There are many ways to allocate this variable, but the HEX directive works nicely:

```
BCDScore        hex 000000
```

We also need a pointer for each of the six digits:

```
Digit0          word
Digit1          word
Digit2          word
Digit3          word
Digit4          word
Digit5          word
```

We will also use a lookup table for the bitmaps of digits 0-9. Timing is critical, so we need to use ALIGN to make sure it doesn't cross a page boundary (we can also save an addition if we know the low byte is zero):

```
        align $100 ; make sure data doesn't cross page boundary
FontTable
        hex 003c6666766e663c007e181818381818
        hex 007e60300c06663c003c66061c06663c
        hex 0006067f661e0e06003c6606067c607e
        hex 003c66667c60663c00181818180c667e
        hex 003c66663c66663c003c66063e66663c
```

Now we need to set up the six Digit pointers. Each byte of the score contains two BCD digits, so we'll need to extract the high nibble and low nibble separately, then multiply each by 8 to arrive at the offset for each digit's pointer:

```
GetDigitPtrs subroutine
        ldx #0   ; leftmost bitmap
        ldy #2   ; start from most-sigificant BCD value
.Loop
        lda BCDScore,y   ; get BCD value
        and #$f0         ; isolate high nibble (* 16)
        lsr              ; shift right 1 bit (* 8)
        sta Digit0,x     ; store pointer lo byte
        lda #>FontTable
        sta Digit0+1,x   ; store pointer hi byte
        inx
        inx              ; next bitmap pointer
        lda BCDScore,y   ; get BCD value (again)
        and #$f          ; isolate low nibble
        asl
        asl
        asl              ; * 8
        sta Digit0,x     ; store pointer lo byte
        lda #>FontTable
        sta Digit0+1,x   ; store pointer hi byte
        inx
        inx              ; next bitmap pointer
        dey              ; next BCD value
        bpl .Loop        ; repeat until < 0
        rts
```

The kernel loop is similar to previous 48-pixel kernels, except it uses the (aa),y indirect addressing mode:

```
; Display the resulting 48x8 bitmap
; using the Digit0-5 pointers.
DrawDigits subroutine
        sta WSYNC
        SLEEP 40          ; start near end of scanline
        lda #7
        sta LoopCount
BigLoop
        ldy LoopCount     ; counts backwards
        lda (Digit0),y    ; load B0 (1st sprite byte)
        sta GRP0          ; B0 -> [GRP0]
        lda (Digit1),y    ; load B1 -> A
        sta GRP1          ; B1 -> [GRP1], B0 -> GRP0
        sta WSYNC         ; sync to next scanline
        lda (Digit2),y    ; load B2 -> A
        sta GRP0          ; B2 -> [GRP0], B1 -> GRP1
        lda (Digit5),y    ; load B5 -> A
        sta Temp          ; B5 -> temp
        lda (Digit4),y    ; load B4
        tax               ; -> X
        lda (Digit3),y    ; load B3 -> A
        ldy Temp          ; load B5 -> Y
        sta GRP1          ; B3 -> [GRP1]; B2 -> GRP0
        stx GRP0          ; B4 -> [GRP0]; B3 -> GRP1
        sty GRP1          ; B5 -> [GRP1]; B4 -> GRP0
        sta GRP0          ; ?? -> [GRP0]; B5 -> GRP1
        dec LoopCount     ; go to next line
        bpl BigLoop       ; repeat until < 0

        lda #0            ; clear the sprite registers
        sta GRP0
        sta GRP1
        sta GRP0
        sta GRP1
        rts
```

We also need a subroutine that adds to the score. This routine adds three BCD-encoded bytes to the BCDScore variable, doing the appropriate thing with the carry bits:

```
; Adds value to 6-BCD-digit score.
; A = 1st BCD pair (rightmost)
; X = 2nd BCD pair
; Y = 3rd BCD pair (leftmost)
AddScore subroutine
        sed      ; enter BCD mode
        clc      ; clear carry
        sta Temp
        lda BCDScore
        adc Temp
        sta BCDScore
        stx Temp
        lda BCDScore+1
        adc Temp
        sta BCDScore+1
        sty Temp
        lda BCDScore+2
        adc Temp
        sta BCDScore+2
        cld      ; exit BCD mode
        rts
```

25

A Big Moveable Sprite

The trick to creating a big (48-pixel), moveable sprite is similar to the Asynchronous Playfields (Chapter 21) trick, in that we reprogram the TIA registers on-the-fly, writing to each register multiple times during the scanline. But unlike the playfield, sprites can be moved horizontally. That means we have to time our register writes differently depending on the sprite's horizontal position.

In the past, we've used loops for this, but our tightest loop takes up five cycles for DEY/DEX and BNE instructions. We'd like to be able to get single-cycle precision delays.

To get precise variable timing, we'll rely on a CPU programming technique called a *clockslide* to waste a precise number of cycles. This is a sequence of instructions that looks like this:

```
c9 c9           cmp #$c9
c9 c9           cmp #$c9
c9 c9           cmp #$c9
                ; repeat many times ...
c5 ea           cmp $ea
```

What's so special about these exact instructions? Well, it turns out that CMP #$c9 assembles to c9 c9, so we're creating a big list of #$c9 bytes, followed by a c5 ea (CMP $ea). This sequence is carefully crafted so that you can start the instruction pointer at any byte, even inside of an instruction, and it will waste cycles proportional to the distance from the end. Let's say we start execution six bytes from the end:

```
c9 c9        cmp #$c9        2
c9 c9        cmp #$c9        2
c5 ea        cmp $ea         3
```

We decode two CMP #$c9 instructions, which take two cycles each, and one CMP $ea, which takes three cycles, for a total of seven cycles. Since they are all CMP instructions, there are no side effects besides modifying flags.

Now, what if we started five bytes from the end? Since our instructions take up two bytes each, we'd be essentially starting in the *middle* of an instruction! But the CPU doesn't see the boundaries of our assembler instructions – it will happily execute whatever it sees. This is what it sees:

```
c9 c9        cmp #$c9        2
c9 c5        cmp #$c5        2
ea           nop             2
```

Note that the CMP #$c9 is the same, since we started in the sea of $c9 bytes. But the last two instructions we decode are different. Our last instruction is a NOP, which came from the $ea in the CMP $ea instruction. The NOP only takes two cycles, so we've wasted a total of six cycles, one less than the previous run.

Let's see what would happen if we started four bytes from the end:

```
c9 c9        cmp #$c9        2
c5 ea        cmp $ea         3
```

We're back in alignment with our original assembler code, and this time we take up five cycles – one less than previously.

Using the clockslide is pretty simple, you just compute a pointer to somewhere inside the array depending on how many cycles you want to waste, then do an indirect jump to the pointer:

```
lda #<ClockslideEnd
sec
sbc DelayCycles
sta DelayPtr
lda #>ClockslideEnd
sbc #0
sta DelayPtr+1
jmp (DelayPtr)
```

We're computing the target jump address by subtracting the desired number of delay cycles from the end address.

```
        REPEAT 36
        .byte $c9
        REPEND
        .byte $c9,$c5
ClockslideEnd
        nop
```

Note that we are taking advantage of the REPEAT/REPEND assembler directives to succinctly create an array of 36 $c9 bytes (i.e. 18 CMP #$c9 instructions).

Now we can get to the business of drawing the sprite. The kernel in Figure 25.1 is "WSYNC-free," which means we'll have to make sure it takes exactly 76 cycles. This ensures that the TIA clock starts at the same position at the start of every loop iteration, which ensures that our register writes happen at the exact same moment for every scanline. We'll use the clockslide immediately before entering the kernel loop. Note that we also use the indirect (aa),y addressing mode as shown in the code that follows.

```
.KernelLoop
                nop
                nop
                nop
                ldy     LineCount
                lda     (Data0),Y
                sta     GRP0
                lda     (Data1),Y
                sta     GRP1
                lda     (Data2),Y
                sta     GRP0
                lda     (Data5),Y
                sta     Temp
                lda     (Data4),Y
                tax
                lda     (Data3),Y
                ldy     Temp
                sta     GRP1
                stx     GRP0
                sty     GRP1
                sta     GRP0
                dec     LineCount
                bpl     .KernelLoop
```

Figure 25.1: WSYNC-Free Big Sprite Kernel

26

Sprite Formations

We've seen that we can have a total of five moveable objects on a given scanline – two players, two missiles, and a ball.

We've also seen how the NUSIZ registers can be set to display one, two, or three copies of an object at different spacings. So if we displayed three copies of both player objects, we'd have six objects per scanline (this is how *Space Invaders* works). Now we're going to take advantage of a quirk of this feature to display even more objects on a scanline.

This *sprite retrigger trick* relies on a behavior when the NUSIZ register is set to display multiple copies of objects (usually two).

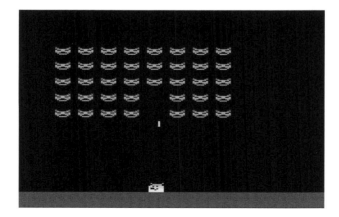

Figure 26.1: Sprite retriggering example game

Basically, if the RESPx register is strobed multiple times on a given scanline, the first (leftmost) copy of the object will be hidden, and the TIA will draw the other copy. You can keep strobing the register to output multiple copies on the same scanline.

The Grid Kernel that draws a single row of evenly-spaced sprites looks like this:

```
KernelLoop
        lda EnemyFrame0,y        ; load bitmap
        sta WSYNC
        ldx EnemyColorFrame0,y   ; load color
        sta GRP0
        sta GRP1
        stx COLUP0
        stx COLUP1
        ldx #0                   ; so we can do the STA RESPn,x variant
KernelStores
        sta RESP0,x
        sta RESP1,x
        sta RESP0,x
        sta RESP1,x
        sta RESP0,x
        sta RESP1,x
        sta RESP0,x
        sta RESP1,x
        dey                      ; also acts as 2-cycle delay
        stx.w GRP0               ; clear player 0 bitmap (4-cycle
    version)
        sta RESP0                ; reset player 0 position
        stx GRP1                 ; clear player 1 bitmap
        sta RESP1                ; reset player 1 position
        bpl KernelLoop           ; repeat until Y < 0
        rts
```

The first instructions at the beginning of KernelLoop look pretty familiar – they are just fetching the bitmap and color data and setting the GRP and COLUP registers for both player objects.

Those eight STA RESPn,x instructions alternately strobe the RESP0 and RESP1 registers exactly four CPU cycles apart (this is the only reason we use the STA aa,x addressing mode). This gives us a spacing of 12 pixels for each sprite. Since we've set the

NUSIZ0 and NUSIZ1 registers to "two copies, close," we'll see the sprite 16 pixels after the write takes place, for a total of eight sprites. Alternating RESP0 and RESP1 gives each sprite enough time to fully draw before it is reset.

The other instructions from the DEY to the BPL clean up, relying on some careful timing to clear the GRP0/GRP1 registers to blank out the sprite, then hitting RESP0/RESP1 again to set up for the next scanline.

But what if we want fewer than eight sprites, or an arbitrary combination of zero to eight sprites? We do not have any cycles to spare to test to check that sprites should or should not exist; we're hitting the RESP0/RESP1 registers as fast as we can.

The only way to get the performance we need is a trick called *self-modifying code*. Our nefarious plan: To copy the entire routine into RAM, surgically replace certain parts of the code, and then jump into RAM to execute our Frankenroutine!

We'll copy the routine into RAM at the start of the program. Before we go to draw a row of sprites, we'll check to see if each of the eight sprites exists by checking a bitmask. If it does, we'll write the appropriate RESP0 ($10) or RESP1 ($11) which matches the original code. If it doesn't exist, we'll write a $30 which points to a read-only register (CXM0P, if you must know) so nothing will happen.

The full routine looks something like this:

```
DrawFormation
        ldx CurRow
        lda EnemyRows0,x
        ldx #1   ; start at KernelStores+1
ShiftLoop
        ldy #RESP0
        ror
        bcs NoClearEnemy0
        ldy #$30           ; no-op
NoClearEnemy0
        sty ZPWrites,x
        inx
        inx
```

```
        ldy #RESP1
        ror
        bcs NoClearEnemy1
        ldy #$30            ; no-op
NoClearEnemy1
        sty ZPWrites,x
        inx
        inx
        cpx #16             ; 8*2 bytes
        bcc ShiftLoop
        ldy EnemyColorFrame0    ; get height -> Y
        jsr ZPRoutine           ; draw sprites
        rts
```

We compute the ZPWrites label with an EQU directive, so that if we modify the kernel routine everything will still work correctly:

```
ZPWrites        equ ZPRoutine+(KernelStores-KernelLoop)
```

Note that our Grid Kernel routine does not draw missiles because we just don't have the time. Rather, we set the missile registers before we draw (we actually use the ball register for the player's missile so that it gets its own color). This creates a long stripe whenever the missile is present. If we wanted to draw the missile correctly, we'd have to probably give up the line-by-line sprite color and do something like this:

```
        lda EnemyFrame0,y       ; load bitmap
        sta WSYNC
        sta GRP0
        sta GRP1
        lda MissileData,y       ; load missile data
        sta ENABL
```

In this snippet, MissileData is an array we precompute with either 2 or 0 for each scanline depending on whether the missile should be drawn. But good luck drawing *two* missiles!

There are also a couple of other modifications we can make to this kernel:

- We could add more STA RESPn,x instructions to create more sprites. We could draw up to 11 sprites this way. However, this requires some tricky logic if you want to remove sprites, because we'll have to remove the instructions that reset the sprite at the end of the scanline.
- We could replace the STA WSYNC with a couple of NOPs and make the loop take exactly 76 cycles. Then we could use the Clockslide technique from Chapter 25 to have some control over horizontal position.

This technique is useful for drawing static displays, like a map or grid of tiles. If you need horizontal movement, it's probably a lot easier to just use the NUSIZ registers with two player objects and limit yourself to six sprites per scanline!

Advanced Timer Tricks

We mentioned the PIA timer in Chapter 12 and how it could be used to count exact numbers of scanlines. In some of our kernels, we're doing some pretty complicated logic during the frame and it may be difficult to sprinkle STA WSYNCs around or count CPU cycles. We could actually use the PIA timer to keep track of our scanlines for us.

We just set the PIA timer at the beginning of our frame, as usual:

```
TIMER_SETUP 192
```

And from there, our various routines read the PIA timer (the INTIM register) to figure out which scanline we're on. It's not perfect, because our preferred PIA timer resolution is 64 cycles, and a scanline is every 76 cycles. But it's good enough for our purposes, and a lot more convenient.

For instance, here we wait until it's time to start drawing a row of sprites:

```
WaitForRow
        jsr DrawMissiles        ; set missile registers
        ldx CurRow              ; get current row of sprites
        lda EnemyYpos0,x        ; get row Y position
        cmp INTIM               ; compare to timer
        bcc WaitForRow          ; wait until timer > Y position
```

Note that there's no STA WSYNC here! We just keep calling DrawMissiles (which also uses the timer to see if missiles intersect

137

the current scanline) until the timer counts down below a given value.

We've got to be careful not to let the timer go below zero, though, because at that point it goes negative and our code might miss it. As described in the Stella Programming Guide[4], this is a feature, not a bug, as it allows programmers to determine how long ago the timer expired:

> The PIA decrements the value or count loaded into it once each interval until it reaches 0. It holds that 0 counts for one interval, then the counter flips to $FF and decrements once each clock cycle, rather than once per interval. The purpose of this feature is to allow the programmer to determine how long ago the timer zeroed out in the event the timer was read after it passed zero. (Wright, 1979, Section 2.3)

There are also cases where the timer changes very close to the end of a scanline, and our next WSYNC might miss it. One solution is to always have a constant number of cycles between the point where your timer loop exits and the next WSYNC. You'll then at least miss lines predictably.

For example, the example program for Chapter 26 (Formation Flying at 8bitworkshop.com) has a DrawMissiles routine which is used to draw 8-pixel high missiles using the PIA timer value:

```
DrawMissiles
        lda INTIM        ; load timer value
        pha              ; save timer value
        sec
        sbc MissileY0    ; subtract missile 0's Y from timer
    value
        cmp #8           ; within 8 lines of missile?
        lda #3           ; bit 1 now set
        adc #0           ; if carry set, bit 1 cleared
        sta ENABL        ; enable/disable ball
        pla              ; restore original timer value
        sec
```

```
        sbc MissileY1    ; subtract missile 1's Y from timer
    value
        cmp #8           ; within 8 lines of missile?
        lda #3           ; bit 1 now set
        adc #0           ; if carry set, bit 1 cleared
        sta ENAM1        ; enable/disable missile
        rts
```

Instead of branch instructions, we use the carry bit in the CMP instruction to modify the result of the ADC instruction. If it's clear, we store a three; if it's set, a four. Only the second bit is valid in the ENAxx register, so three enables the object and four disables it. This gives the routine a constant cycle count.

The timer can also be used to implement a simple timeslicing system. If there are optional or partial routines to run in the offscreen periods, you could check the timer to see if there's enough time left before executing. You could split some routines into bite-sized pieces and execute them this way.

27.1 Timer Tables

Since scanlines take 76 CPU cycles and the closest PIA timer period is 64 cycles, we don't have an easy mapping between timer values and scanlines. This diagram shows the problem:

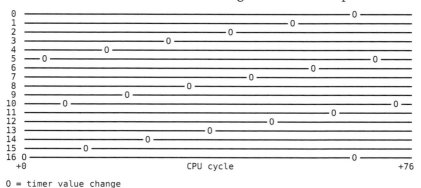

0 = timer value change

Figure 27.1: PIA Timer Scanline Timing

139

All scanlines will span at least two consecutive timer values. This makes it impossible to tell which scanline we're on unless we look for transitions between timer values.

This should work, except when the timer changes very close to the end of the scanline – about 18% of the time. Several CPU cycles will pass between the time we detect the timer change and when we STA WSYNC to sync to the end of the scanline, so it's hard to stop on a precise scanline in this case.

The solution is to have a lookup table that maps timer values to scanlines, except for timer values that change too close (11 cycles) to the edge – these are set to 0. Then whenever we detect a timer change, we immediately WSYNC and then compare the value we lookup in the table to our desired scanline. If we're not there yet, or if the value in the table is zero (meaning "skip it"), we go back and try again. The table has an entry for every scanline from 1 to 215, so we can target any scanline this way.

Here's the routine:

```
;     Pass: A = desired scanline
; Returns: Y = timer value - 1
        align $10
WaitForScanline subroutine
        ldy INTIM       ; Fetch timer value
.Wait
        cpy INTIM
        beq .Wait       ; Wait for it to change
        sta WSYNC       ; Sync with scan line
        cmp Timer2Scanline,y ; lookup scanline
        bcs WaitForScanline  ; repeat until >= desired
        rts
```

This routine requires careful analysis, since we're building a table based on it. All we really care about is how long it takes this routine to get to WSYNC, since at that point we've chosen a scanline. Let's go line-by-line and consider CPU cycles for each instruction:

```
        ldy INTIM       ; 4 (read occurs on last cycle)
.Wait
        cpy INTIM       ; 4
        beq .Wait       ; 2 (3 if branch taken)
        sta WSYNC       ; 3
```

The routine takes at least 13 cycles total, with seven or six (final) cycles spent in each loop iteration. Let's consider the worst-case, where the timer changes value right after the second CPY instruction reads from memory:

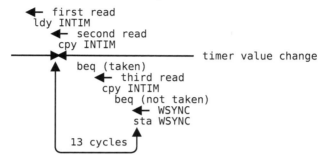

Figure 27.2: Timer worst-case scenario

There are 13 cycles between the second CPY read and the STA WSYNC, so that's our effective resolution. In this case, we need to ensure that we don't enter this critical region in the 13 cycles before the end of a scanline, or we could potentially wrap to the next scanline.

Here's the lookup table:

```
     align $100
Timer2Scanline
    .byte 215,  0,214,213,212,211,210,  0,209,208,207,206,205,204,  0,203
    .byte 202,201,200,199,  0,198,197,196,195,194,  0,193,192,191,190,189
    .byte 188,  0,187,186,185,184,183,  0,182,181,180,179,178,  0,177,176
    .byte 175,174,173,172,  0,171,170,169,168,167,  0,166,165,164,163,162
    .byte   0,161,160,159,158,157,156,  0,155,154,153,152,151,  0,150,149
    .byte 148,147,146,  0,145,144,143,142,141,140,  0,139,138,137,136,135
    .byte   0,134,133,132,131,130,  0,129,128,127,126,125,124,  0,123,122
    .byte 121,120,119,  0,118,117,116,115,114,  0,113,112,111,110,109,108
    .byte   0,107,106,105,104,103,  0,102,101,100, 99, 98,  0, 97, 96, 95
    .byte  94, 93, 92,  0, 91, 90, 89, 88, 87,  0, 86, 85, 84, 83, 82,  0
    .byte  81, 80, 79, 78, 77, 76,  0, 75, 74, 73, 72, 71,  0, 70, 69, 68
    .byte  67, 66,  0, 65, 64, 63, 62, 61, 60,  0, 59, 58, 57, 56, 55,  0
    .byte  54, 53, 52, 51, 50,  0, 49, 48, 47, 46, 45, 44,  0, 43, 42, 41
    .byte  40, 39,  0, 38, 37, 36, 35, 34,  0, 33, 32, 31, 30, 29, 28,  0
    .byte  27, 26, 25, 24, 23,  0, 22, 21, 20, 19, 18,  0, 17, 16, 15, 14
    .byte  13, 12,  0, 11, 10,  9,  8,  7,  0,  6,  5,  4,  3,  2,  0,  1
```

Figure 27.3: Timer-to-Scanline Lookup Table

Note the `align $100` which we use to avoid crossing page boundaries and upsetting the timing.

141

The routine assumes the timer starts at 255, so before using the routine we should set up the timer like this:

```
lda #$ff
sta WSYNC
sta TIM64T
```

Or using the macro:

```
TIMER_SETUP 216
```

Call the routine like this:

```
lda #50
jsr WaitForScanline
```

The routine returns even if we've passed the desired scanline, so if we just want to wait for the next valid scanline, we pass zero:

```
lda #0
jsr WaitForScanline
lda Timer2Scanline,y     ; fetch exact scanline
```

If we don't need precise accuracy, we can also grab the current approximate scanline, which could be off by -1 to +1:

```
; Fetchs the approximate scanline (could be off by +/- 1)
; into A. Takes 11 or 14 cycles.
        MAC GET_APPROX_SCANLINE
        ldy INTIM                ; get timer
        lda Timer2Scanline,y     ; lookup scanline
        bne .Ok                  ; non-zero?
        lda Timer2Scanline-1,y   ; lookup next scanline
.Ok
        ENDM
```

But why go to all this trouble? Well, sometimes we want to do some complex stuff between scanlines and don't want the hassle of tracking each and every one, or we want the freedom to miss a WSYNC or two and not have the rest of the frame be completely goofy. We'll use these routines in Chapter 28 for a complicated multi-sprite kernel.

28

Multisprites

For many games, we'd like to display more than two sprites. Unfortunately, the VCS hardware is really limited to two distinct sprites per scanline, unless you get fancy with the NUSIZ register and other TIA tricks. But if we reprogram the TIA between sprites, we can get more on the screen – even though we're still limited to two sprites on a given scanline.

There are a lot of different ways to tackle this on the VCS, but we're going to try for a generalized approach that allows us to use position sprites at any X-Y coordinate, each with its own bitmap and color table. This is tricky because we can only do so much on each scanline.

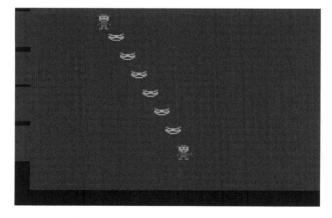

Figure 28.1: Multiple sprites example

143

Our approach is to separate the problem into three phases:

1. Sort vertically
2. Position horizontally
3. Display sprite (then repeat steps 2 and 3)

In the Sort phase, we sort all sprites by Y coordinate. We do one sort pass per frame, so it may take several frames for the sort to stabilize.

In the Position phase, we look at the sprites in Y-sorted order, looking several lines ahead to see if a sprite is coming up. We then allocate it to one of the two TIA's player objects and set its position using the SetHorizPos method. We can set one or both of the player objects this way, one at a time.

In the Display phase, we draw the objects which we previously assigned and positioned. First we figure out how many scanlines are required to draw. For one object, we just go to its bottommost scanline. For two objects, we go to the bottommost scanline of either object.

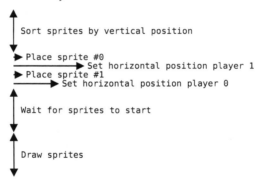

Figure 28.2: Phases

We then loop through the scanlines, fetching pixels and colors for one or both objects (up to four lookup tables) and setting registers at the appropriate time. We don't have time to do much else, so we don't look for any new objects to schedule until we're done with this loop.

This scheme can only display up to two objects on a given scanline, so if the system tries to schedule a third, it will be ignored. Also, the positioning routine takes a few scanlines to complete, so if the top of a sprite is too close to the bottom of another sprite, the latter may not be displayed.

To mitigate this, we increment a priority counter when a sprite entry is missed. In the sort phase, we move those sprites ahead of lower priority sprites in the sort order. This makes overlapping sprites flicker instead of randomly disappear. If all goes well, each sprite will get an equal share of screen time.

28.1 Variables

This routine requires lots of variables in RAM, so let's walk through them. First, we have four arrays which keep track of our sprites, each eight bytes long:

```
NSprites        equ 8       ; max # of sprites
XPos0           ds NSprites ; X coord for each sprite
YPos0           ds NSprites ; Y coord for each sprite
Sorted0         ds NSprites ; sorted list of sprite indices
Priority0       ds NSprites ; sprite priority list, if missed
```

The XPos0 and YPos0 arrays track the coordinates of each sprite (the "0" suffix reminds us that this is the address of the first array element).

The Sorted0 array keeps a list of sprites sorted by vertical position, top-first. Each entry is the index of the sprite (0-7).

Priority0 is an array tracks sprites that are missed – we'll discuss this later.

As we go down the screen, CurIndex keeps track of which sprite to look at next (i.e., which entry of the Sorted0 array):

```
CurIndex byte   ; current sorted sprite # to try to schedule
```

The other variables are used by our sprite kernel, and they keep pointers to bitmap and color tables for each sprite, as well as the positions and heights of the next sprites to draw:

```
PData0   word    ; pointer (lo/hi) to player 0 bitmap data
PColr0   word    ; pointer to player 0 color data
PData1   word    ; pointer to player 1 bitmap data
PColr1   word    ; pointer to player 1 color data
SIndx0   byte    ; next y-position to draw player 0
                 ; or during draw, index into sprite
                 ; zero means not assigned
SIndx1   byte    ; ... for player 1
SSize0   byte    ; sprite size for player 0 (0 = inactive)
SSize1   byte    ; sprite size for player 1
```

28.2 Position

In the Position step, we try to assign the next sprite in the sort order to one of the two player objects. FindAnotherSprite is the subroutine that does this:

```
FindAnotherSprite
        GET_APPROX_SCANLINE
        clc
        adc #MinYDist
        sta Scanline
```

We use the GET_APPROX_SCANLINE macro as discussed in Chapter 27 to see which approximate scanline we're currently drawing, plus or minus one. We bias it with MinYDist (+7) because that's the maximum number of lines we can afford to spend before moving to the Display phase. Then, we check the next sprite in the sort sequence to make sure we won't miss it:

```
        ldx CurIndex
        cpx #NSprites
        bcs .OutOfSprites ; no more sprites to check
        ldy Sorted0,x    ; get sprite index # in Y-sorted order
        lda YPos0,y      ; get Y position of sprite
        cmp Scanline     ; SpriteY - Scanline
        bmi .MissedSprite ; passed it? (or > 127 lines away)
```

Now that a sprite is starting soon, we need to schedule it to one or the other of the player objects. First, we check player 1:

```
lda XPos0,y
ldx SIndx1          ; player 1 available?
bne .Plyr1NotReady  ; no, try player 0
```

Due to timing issues, we have artifacts if player 1 is too close to the left edge of the screen. This is a problem. Many VCS programming solutions require the type of wisdom you get from an old vaudeville sketch: "Doc, it hurts when I do this." "Well, don't *do* that!"

One solution is to just not allow player 1's sprite to get too far to the left.

TIP: To run and modify an example that shows multiple sprites in action, check out the Multiple Sprites sample available at 8bitworkshop.com. Use the arrow keys to move the sprite (and move to the left to see the too-close-to-the-edge issue in action!).

We try to put those sprites in the player 0 slot:

```
cmp #34            ; X < 34
bcc .Plyr1NotReady
```

Whichever player object we pick, the first step is to set the sprite's horizontal offset using the SetHorizPos subroutine – this could use up to two scanlines:

```
ldx #1             ; player 1 object
jsr SetHorizPos ; set horizontal position (does WSYNC)
```

Then, we set various variables for the player 1 sprite, including Y position, pointers to bitmap and color maps, and set the height of the sprite:

```
        lda YPos0,y
        sta SIndx1
; Get index into SpriteDataMap (index * 4)
        ldx MultBy4,y
; Copy addresses of pixel/color maps to player 1
        lda SpriteDataMap,x
        sta PData1
        lda SpriteDataMap+1,x
        sta PData1+1
        lda SpriteDataMap+2,x
        sta PColr1
        lda SpriteDataMap+3,x
        sta PColr1+1
; Get the sprite height as the first byte of the color map
        ldy #0
        lda (PColr1),y
        sta SSize1
        jmp .SetupDone
```

There's a similar routine to set up the player 0 sprite.

28.3   Display

After we set up the sprites, we now enter the display phase. First we use the WaitForScanline subroutine as described in Chapter 27 to wait for an exact scanline. We pass it zero, which makes it wait for the next scanline that can be measured, and returns its value in A:

```
DrawSprites subroutine
        lda #0                 ; 0 = wait for next
        jsr WaitForScanline
        lda Timer2Scanline,y ; lookup scanline #
        sta Scanline           ; save it
```

Next, we calculate how many scanlines need to be drawn for each sprite, starting at the current scanline.

```
        lda SIndx0
        beq .Empty0      ; sprite 0 is inactive?
        sec
        sbc Scanline
        clc
        adc SSize0
        sta SIndx0       ; SIndx0 += SSize0 - Scanline
.Empty0
        lda SIndx1
        beq .Empty1      ; sprite 1 is inactive?
        sec
        sbc Scanline
        clc
        adc SSize1
        sta SIndx1       ; SIndx1 += SSize1 - Scanline
.Empty1
```

Now that we have the scanline counts for each player, we take the maximum value, and that's the total number of lines to draw (if it's zero, that means there weren't any sprites to draw):

```
        cmp SIndx0
        bpl .Cmp1        ; sindx0 < sindx1?
        lda SIndx0
.Cmp1
        tax              ; X = # of lines left to draw
        beq .NoSprites   ; X = 0? we're done
        sta WSYNC        ; next scanline
```

The main sprite-drawing loop should be pretty familiar – it first draws player 0:

```
.DrawNextScanline
; Make sure player 0 index is within bounds
        ldy SIndx0
        cpy SSize0
        bcs .Inactive0   ; index >= size? (or index < 0)
; Lookup pixels for player 0
        lda (PData0),y
; Do WSYNC and then quickly store pixels for player 0
        sta WSYNC
        sta GRP0
```

149

```
; Lookup/store colors for player 0
        lda (PColr0),y
        sta COLUP0
```

There's an alternate player 0 path when this sprite is inactive:

```
.Inactive0
        sta WSYNC
        lda #0
        sta GRP0
        sta COLUP0
        beq .DrawSprite1 ; always taken due to lda #0
```

And then we draw player 1, with the understanding that we might be up to 34 pixels (about 36 CPU cycles) into the scanline by the time it finishes writing to registers. This is why the FindAnotherSprite routine doesn't put sprites that are close to the left side of the screen in the player 1 slot.

```
.DrawSprite1
; Make sure player 1 index is within bounds
        ldy SIndx1
        cpy SSize1
        bcs .Inactive1  ; index >= size? (or index < 0)
; Lookup/store pixels and colors for player 1
; Note that we are already 30-40 pixels into the scanline
; by this point...
        lda (PData1),y
        sta GRP1
        lda (PColr1),y
        sta COLUP1
```

Now we just repeat the loop, decrementing the various indices:

```
.Inactive1
        dey
        sty SIndx1
        dec SIndx0
```

Repeat until we've drawn all the scanlines for this job:

```
        dex
        bne .DrawNextScanline
```

At the end, we free up both player slots by zeroing them out, as well as cleaning up the player registers:

```
        stx SIndx0
        stx SIndx1
        stx SSize0
        stx SSize1
        sta WSYNC
        stx GRP0
        stx GRP1
.NoSprites
        rts
```

28.4 The Main Loop

The main kernel loop relies on the timer functions in Chapter 12, so the first thing we do is set up the timer:

```
TIMER_SETUP 216 ; timer <- #$ff
lda #$90
sta COLUBK
```

The main loop starts by calling FindAnotherSprite twice, which tries to schedule the next two sprites in the sort order to player slots:

```
NextFindSprite
        jsr FindAnotherSprite
        jsr FindAnotherSprite
```

We defer the WSYNC and HMOVE so we can do them both at once (if two sprites were scheduled) which saves us a scanline:

```
        sta WSYNC        ; start next scanline
        sta HMOVE        ; apply the previous fine position(s)
```

Now we draw any sprites that have been scheduled:

```
        jsr DrawSprites
```

We strobe HMCLR to erase any previous fine offsets, and then we check INTIM (the timer) to see if we're far enough down the

screen to finish the loop. If so, we call WaitForScanline so that
we end the loop on a known scanline.

```
sta HMCLR          ; reset the old horizontal position(s)
lda INTIM
cmp #$14           ; scanline 198
bcs NextFindSprite
lda #201           ; + 9 lines, end exactly
jsr WaitForScanline
```

28.5   Sort

The sort routine is called during the VBLANK period. It's a bubble
sort algorithm, which is pretty simple to implement. The idea
is that you compare successive pairs of entries, and swap them
until they are in order. We just sort the Sorted0 array, not all four
object arrays. The pseudocode looks like this:

```
if Priority[i] < Priority[i+1]:
        Priority[i] = Priority[i+1] = 0
        Swap Sorted[i], Sorted[i+1]
else if Y[i] >= Y[i+1]:
        Swap Sorted[i], Sorted[i+1]
```

We run this for each pair of sprite indices – e.g. if there are 8
sprites, we run it for indices 0 through 6 (which swap with 1
through 7).

The 6502 code is not very complicated, just a bunch of indexed
lookups, comparisons, loads, and stores:

```
; Perform one sort iteration
; X register contains sort index (0 to NSprites-1)
SwapSprites
; First compare Priority[i] and Priority[i+1]
        lda Priority0,x
        cmp Priority0+1,x
        bcs NoPrioritySwap
; If Priority[i] < Priority[i+1], do the swap
; anyway after resetting priorities
        lda #0
        sta Priority0,x
        sta Priority0+1,x       ; reset
```

```
        ldy Sorted0+1,x
        bcc DoSwap       ; swap due to priority
NoPrioritySwap
; Compare Y[i] and Y[i+1]
        ldy Sorted0,x
        lda YPos0,y
        ldy Sorted0+1,x
        cmp YPos0,y
        bcc NoSwap       ; Y[i] < Y[i+1]? don't swap
DoSwap
; Swap Sorted[i] and Sorted[i+1]
        lda Sorted0,x    ; A <- Sorted[i]
        sty Sorted0,x    ; Y -> Sorted[i]
        sta Sorted0+1,x  ; A -> Sorted[i+1]
NoSwap
        rts
```

28.6 Improvements

- Our timing is heavily constrained here by our insistence on using single-height bitmap and color tables, which requires we update four registers on every scanline. If we used double-height tables we would only have to update two registers per line, but our sprites would have half the vertical resolution.
- We also are still using WSYNC to find the beginning of the next scanline, but in really optimized kernels we carefully analyze our code so that each loop iteration takes exactly 76 CPU cycles, or one scanline. (We made such a kernel in Chapter 25.)
- Our priority-based sorting algorithm works OK, but has some weird flickers at times. It also uses too much memory; we could combine the Sorted0 array with the Priority0 array (since they both need less than 8 bits) at the expense of extra CPU cycles.
- You might notice that there are 8-pixel wide black bands on the left edge of the screen. These are artifacts caused by the HMOVE register strobe. If you have a black background, you won't see this problem. Some Activision games worked around it by strobing HMOVE after every WSYNC, whether or not it was needed.

29

Random Number Generation

Most games have a need to generate random numbers. Maybe the game needs an enemy that behaves unpredictably, or requires that a game element appears at random positions on the screen. This is usually accomplished by using a *pseudorandom number generator* (PRNG). This is an algorithm that starts from a number called a *seed* and modifies it in a complex way to generate successive random numbers.

If designed correctly, the PRNG will cycle through a large range of values that seemingly do not repeat themselves, or only repeat after many thousands of iterations. This is called the *period* of the PRNG.

A common type of PRNG is a *linear-feedback shift register (LFSR)* which combines shifts with bit operations to generate numbers. The operations are usually carefully chosen to maximize the period of the sequence. For math reasons, only 16 different 8-bit LFSRs have the maximal period of 255 values (zero is not allowed, otherwise it'd be 256). This means it'll cycle through every non-zero 8-bit number exactly once, in a seemingly haphazard order, until it repeats.

Because memory is so scarce on the Atari 2600, many games use LFSRs to generate random worlds for a game instead of a map stored in the ROM. This is often called *procedural generation*. As long as the game starts with the same seed, the sequence of numbers will be predictable (*deterministic*) and all players will see the same level.

For example, in the classic Activision game *Pitfall!*, the bits in the generated numbers correspond to features of the room – whether it has a pit, vine, etc. In *River Raid*, they are used to generate the countours and obstacles in a infinitely scrolling river course. Since the LFSR eventually cycles through every value, every possible combination of features will be seen if the game plays through long enough.

The type of LFSR used in these games is called a *Fibonacci LFSR*, and it is computed like this:

```
lda     Random
asl
eor     Random
asl
eor     Random
asl
asl
eor     Random
asl
rol     Random
```

A handy property of some LFSRs is that they can be reversed. This is used in *Pitfall!* when the player exits a room to the left. This code reverses the effect of the previous routine:

```
lda     Random
asl
eor     Random
asl
eor     Random
asl
asl
rol
eor     Random
lsr
ror     Random
```

There is another type of LFSR called a *Galois LFSR* which is even more compact:

```
        lda Random
        lsr
        bcc .NoEor
        eor #$d4        ; #%11010100
.NoEor:
        sta Random
```

We used $D4 in our example, but other constants that give you the full range of 255 unique numbers include: $8E, $95, $96, $A6, $AF, $B1, $B2, $B4, $B8, $C3, $C6, $D4, $E1, $E7, $F3, and $FA.

The inverse is just as simple, we just have to shift left instead of right, and use a different constant (the original constant rotated left 1 bit):

```
        lda Random
        asl
        bcc .NoEor
        eor #$a9        ; #%10101001
.NoEor:
        sta Random
```

Since half of the time a Galois LFSR just performs a simple shift, you may have to iterate them at least twice to get plausible-looking random values. Because the period of a maximal LFSR is odd, you can iterate twice and still get the full range of values.

You can also extend a Galois LFSR to 16 bits. It's pretty much the same as the 8-bit version, except we use the 16-bit constant $d400:

```
        lsr Random+1
        ror Random
        bcc .NoEor
        lda Random+1
        eor #$d4
        sta Random+1
.NoEor:
        rts
```

And the reverse, which uses the constant $a801 (the previous constant rotated left by 1 bit):

```
        asl Random
        rol Random+1
        bcc .NoEor
        lda Random
        eor #$01
        sta Random
        lda Random+1
        eor #$a8
        sta Random+1
.NoEor:
        rts
```

These "magic numbers" give us the full range of values (255 for the 8-bit version and 65,535 for the 16-bit version) but other constants will result in shorter periods. LFSRs are also used in the TIA chip to generate sound, and we'll see that they are configurable in a similar way.

Another cheap source of pseudo-randomness is to just read bytes from the code in the ROM directly, say starting at $F000. This is sometimes used to provide noisy backgrounds, since the pattern of bytes is usually random enough to trick the eye. It's not great for procedural generation, though, because many values will be over- or under-represented.

30

Procedural Generation

We learned how to use LFSRs to generate sequences of pseudo-random numbers – now let's put them to use. We're going to build a random series of rooms that the player can walk through.

We'll use an 8-bit value to track the room number, just like *Pitfall!*. As the player moves from room to room, we'll use the LFSR to modify the number. The rooms will look like they're random, but the player will be able to revisit old rooms and they'll look the same.

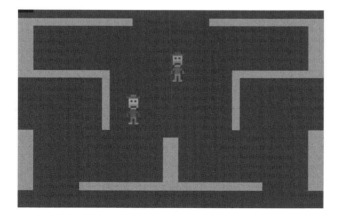

Figure 30.1: Procedurally-generated room

> **TIP:** To access an example with the sample code described in this chapter, access the Procedural Generation example available at 8bitworkshop.com. Not only can you modify the code and see your changes in real-time, but you can also use arrow keys to navigate rooms!

We'll use a Galois LFSR (as described in the last chapter) to modify the value forward and backward:

```
NextRandom SUBROUTINE
        lsr
        bcc .NoEor
        eor #$d4
.NoEor:
        rts
PrevRandom SUBROUTINE
        asl
        bcc .NoEor
        eor #$a9
.NoEor:
        rts
```

We'll start at room number 1. When we move down off the bottom of the screen, we'll go to the next room number by iterating the LFSR two times. When we move up, we'll go to the previous room by reverse-iterating two times. Going left and right will teleport seven rooms back or seven rooms forward.

These routines will handle changing rooms, using the Y register to count moving by multiple rooms:

```
MoveNextRoom
        lda RoomType
        jsr NextRandom
        dey
        sta RoomType
        bne MoveNextRoom
        rts
MovePrevRoom
        lda RoomType
        jsr PrevRandom
        dey
        sta RoomType
        bne MovePrevRoom
        rts
```

We'll use the bits of the room number to define where walls will be in the room. The plan is to divide the playfield into three sections:

- Top (3x2 playfield bytes)
- Middle (3x3 playfield bytes)
- Bottom (3x2 playfield bytes)

We'll store various "wall components" in tables, and use the bits of the room number to index into these tables. The first two bits are used to choose between four different top sections:

```
BuildRoom
        lda RoomType
        and #3
        jsr MulBy3ToX
        lda PFRoomTop0+0,x
        sta PFData+0
        lda PFRoomTop0+1,x
        sta PFData+1
        lda PFRoomTop0+2,x
        sta PFData+2
        lda PFRoomTop1+0,x
        sta PFData+3
        lda PFRoomTop1+1,x
        sta PFData+4
        lda PFRoomTop1+2,x
        sta PFData+5
```

Then the next two bits are used for the middle:

```
        lda RoomType
        ror
        ror
        and #3
        jsr MulBy3ToX
        lda PFRoomMid0+0,x
        sta PFData+6
        lda PFRoomMid0+1,x
        sta PFData+7
        lda PFRoomMid0+2,x
        sta PFData+8
        lda PFRoomMid1+0,x
        sta PFData+9
        lda PFRoomMid1+1,x
```

```
sta PFData+10
lda PFRoomMid1+2,x
sta PFData+11
lda PFRoomMid2+0,x
sta PFData+12
lda PFRoomMid2+1,x
sta PFData+13
lda PFRoomMid2+2,x
sta PFData+14
```

The bottom section is the reflection of the top section of the next room, so that the openings match up. (The left and right rooms will always have compatible openings.) We can easily call NextRandom to fetch the next room's value:

```
lda RoomType
jsr NextRandom
pha
and #3
jsr MulBy3ToX
lda PFRoomTop1+0,x
sta PFData+15
lda PFRoomTop1+1,x
sta PFData+16
lda PFRoomTop1+2,x
sta PFData+17
lda PFRoomTop0+0,x
sta PFData+18
lda PFRoomTop0+1,x
sta PFData+19
lda PFRoomTop0+2,x
sta PFData+20
```

We also set the room colors, using this room's number, and since we've already got it, the next room's number:

```
lda RoomType
and #$f0
sta COLUBK      ; background color
pla             ; next random value, stored
ora #$08
sta COLUPF      ; foreground color
rts
```

We use this subroutine to multiply A by three, because each row of the playfield is three bytes long:

```
MulBy3ToX
        sta Temp
        asl             ; X*2
        clc
        adc Temp        ; (X*2)+X
        tax             ; -> X
        rts
```

Then we'll display the playfield using the two-line kernel as described in Chapter 16, but we'll use another table that maps a section of the screen into the 21 bytes that define the room. We'll call this routine every time we need a new playfield byte:

```
FetchPlayfield
        dec PFOfs
        ldx PFOfs
        ldy PFOffsets,x ; get index into PFData array
        lda PFData,y    ; load playfield byte
        rts
```

That's pretty much it, though we can add a collision routine that makes the player stop when hitting walls. It does this by detecting a collision between player and playfield, and if one is detected it sets the player to its previous position – so the player appears to "wiggle" between frames:

```
; Did the player collide with the wall?
        bit CXP0FB
        bpl NoCollision
; Yes, load previous position
        lda YPosPrev
        sta YPos0
        lda XPosPrev
        sta XPos0
        jmp NoMoveJoy
NoCollision
; No collision, update previous position and move player
        lda YPos0
        sta YPosPrev
        lda XPos0
        sta XPosPrev
        jsr MoveJoystick
```

Drawing Lines

One thing the VCS wasn't really designed for (among many, many other things) is drawing arbitrary lines. But nothing's stopped us yet, so we're going to draw some. There are times when a line comes in handy, like the vine in *Pitfall!*, or the proton beams in *Ghostbusters*.

We're going to define a line by four components: Its starting and ending Y coordinate, its starting X coordinate, and a slope:

```
X1        .byte    ; start X coordinate of line
Y1        .byte    ; start Y coordinate of line
Y2        .byte    ; end Y coordinate of line
Slope     .word    ; 16-bit slope
```

The slope is a 16-bit *fixed-point* quantity. This means that we treat some of the bits in the value as fractional. In this case, we consider the entire lower byte to be $1/256^{th}$ of its integer value.

Figure 31.1: A line drawn with player objects

165

It's like putting an invisible decimal point between each 8 bits of the 16-bit value, i.e. between the two bytes.

```
HiByte    LoByte
-------- --------                N = integer part
NNNNNNNN.xxxxxxx                 x = fractional part
```

Since the slope is fractional, we'll need to track the fractional part of the line's X position:

```
XFrac   .byte            ; X fractional part
```

Before we draw anything, we set up the initial horizontal position of the missile 0 object, which we'll use to draw the line:

```
        lda X1           ; starting X
        ldx #2           ; missile 0
        jsr SetHorizPos
        sta WSYNC
        sta HMOVE        ; apply fine offsets
```

From now on, we're going to use the HMOVE registers to move the missile, so we don't need to actually track its X coordinate in memory. We'll look up the HMOVE values in a table that range from -7 to +8 pixels (as seen in Figure 9.1):

```
HMoveTable
        hex 7060504030201000f0e0d0c0b0a09080
```

We also have a table that defines the width of the missile for each X movement. If the X coordinate moves by just -1, 0, or +1 in a scanline, we keep the missile just 1 pixel wide. If it moves more than that, we progressively expand it to make the line look solid.

```
DotWidths
        hex 40403030201000000010203030404040
```

We track the Y position in the Y register starting at 0. The first step in the loop is to see if we're within the upper and lower Y values:

```
        ldy #0
        sty XFrac          ; reset X fractional part
ScanLoop
        cpy Y1
        bcc NoLine         ; out of bounds (< Y1)?
        cpy Y2
        bcs NoLine         ; out of bounds (> Y2)?
```

The NoLine branch just does a WSYNC, hides the missile, and goes to the next scanline:

```
NoLine
        sta WSYNC
        lda #0
        sta ENAM0          ; hide missile
        jmp NextScan
```

Then we add the fixed-point slope to the X fractional coordinate:

```
        lda XFrac
        clc
        adc Slope          ; this sets carry flag
        sta XFrac
```

The Carry flag will be set if the X fractional part exceeds 255. Now we add the high byte of the slope to the Carry flag, plus 7 so that we can index our two tables:

```
        lda Slope+1
        adc #7             ; 7 + carry flag
        tax                ; -> X
```

Now we can index our two tables. One looks up the HMOVE value so we can move the missile, and the other looks up the width of the missile so we have a solid-looking line if we move more than 1 pixel:

```
        lda DotWidths,x         ; lookup register for missile
width
        sta Temp                ; -> Temp
        lda HMoveTable,x        ; lookup HMOVE register for X
offset
```

Now we WSYNC and apply the register values, and also enable the missile in case it is hidden. Note that we HMOVE before we set the HMM0 register – this is because we want to delay the line's movement until the next scanline, so that the missile's width fills up the gap:

```
NextScan
        sta WSYNC
        sta HMOVE       ; apply moves on previous scanline
        ldx #2
        stx ENAM0       ; enable missile
        ldx Temp
        stx NUSIZ0      ; set missile width
        sta HMM0        ; set HMM0 for next scanline
```

Now we increment Y and repeat until we're out of scanlines:

```
        iny
        cpy #192
        bcc ScanLoop    ; any more scanlines?
        beq DoneLine    ; branch always taken
```

Note that we can't draw near-horizontal lines with this scheme – we can't move a missile more than 8 pixels in a single scanline, and we can't make the missile more than 8 pixels wide.

Our routine has only got about 10 cycles left to do other stuff. For a more time-efficient routine, we'd move the Y bounds check and missile enable/disable out of the loop.

If we didn't need slopes greater than 45 degrees, we'd could take out the table lookups and just use a predetermined HMOVE value,

since each scanline would move either 0 or 1 pixel. *Pitfall!* uses
a simplified routine that does something like this:

```
    lda     XFrac
    clc
    adc     Slope
    sta     XFrac           ; add slope to X fractional part
    lda     #0
    sta     HMCLR           ; clear HMOVE registers
    bcc     .noMove
    lda     HMoveDir        ; HMOVE direction, either #$10 or #$f0
.noMove:
    sta     HMM0            ; store HMOVE register
```

To run and manipulate a line drawing and animation example,
check out the Drawing Lines sample available at 8bitwork-
shop.com.

32

The Sound and Music

Generating sound and music on the VCS is a bit tricky. Because RAM and ROM space is limited, fine control of frequency (pitch) is limited, which requires us to perform some gymnastics to compose VCS-compliant tunes.

The TIA chip in the VCS supports two sound channels, which means it can play two sounds simultaneously. Each channel has three different registers to tweak, which are:

- **Volume** (AUDVx) - Can be set from 0 (off) to 15 (loudest).
- **Control** (AUDCx) - Controls the type of tone, or *distortion*, which varies from pure tones to noise to buzzing sounds. Tone can also be set using values between 0 and 15, though some values are duplicates.
- **Frequency** (AUDFx) - Determines pitch, the range of which varies depending on tone settings. Frequency can be set from 0 (highest pitch) to 31 (lowest pitch).

The different tones are output by a circuit called a polynomial counter, also known as a *pseudorandom shift register*. These nifty little circuits are heavily used in the TIA chip because they require fewer transistors to implement than a binary counter. In the case of sound generation, they also can be configured to output interesting noises. The shift registers emit a stream of binary 0s and 1s (before volume is applied), but changing the tone varies the complexity of the waveform – from simple (like the pure tone modes) to complex (like white noise).

Hex Addr	Name	Bits Used 76543210	Description
15	AUDC0	xxxx	Audio Control Channel 0
16	AUDC1	xxxx	Audio Control Channel 1
17	AUDF0	...xxxxx	Audio Frequency Channel 0
18	AUDF1	...xxxxx	Audio Frequency Channel 1
19	AUDV0	xxxx	Audio Volume Channel 0
1A	AUDV1	xxxx	Audio Volume Channel 1

Table 32.1: Sound Registers

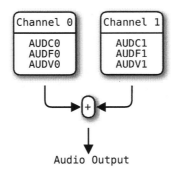

Figure 32.1: Audio Channels to Output

Values	Description	Base Frequency (Hz)
0,11	Silent	
8	White noise	
4,5	Pure tone	15720
12,13	Pure tone	5240
1	Buzz	2096
6,10	Square wave	1014.2
7,9	Buzz	1014.2
14	Square wave	338.1
15	Buzz	338.1
2,3	Rumble	67.6

Table 32.2: Audio Control Register Settings

The Base Frequency column shows the highest frequency possible for each tone, i.e., when the pitch register is set to 0. This value acts as a frequency divider, so a pitch value of 1 divides the frequency by 2, a value of 2 divides by 3, and so on.

The exact frequencies heard by the ear depend on the waveform output by the shift register. For example, Tones 14 and 15 have the same base frequency, but Tone 15 sounds one or two octaves higher because it has more harmonics.

Most of the tones are based on the TIA pixel clock (3.579545 MHz) except for Tones 12-15 which are based on the CPU clock (divide TIA clock by 3, or 1.193182 MHz).

Since each channel only has 32 distinct values to configure pitch, playing music can be challenging as the frequencies rarely line up with the desired notes of a musical scale, and if they do, they're likely out of tune. The best results often come from VCS-specific compositions. Online tools are available to optimally match musical notes to VCS register values; check out webTune2600[6].

We can update the sound registers at any time and the change takes effect immediately. It's usually sufficient to only update them once per frame, i.e., every $1/60^{th}$ second on NTSC.

32.1 Music Player

Our score (the encoded representation of the music) consists of three types of objects: Tracks, patterns, and notes.

There are two tracks, one for each audio channel. Each track consists of a list of patterns, each entry being a byte offset into the Patterns array.

A pattern is a list of variable-length notes, each of which is defined by a pitch and duration.

The patterns in the tracks are played in-order until one ends, and then both tracks are restarted. It's up to the composer to make sure that the durations in each track line up properly.

Patterns consist of NOTE or TONE commands. TONE sets the tone of the channel (the AUDCx register) and NOTE plays a note with a duration taken from a lookup table. TONE 0 ends a pattern.

Notes have the following format:

- lower 5 bits - pitch
- upper 3 bits - duration

If duration is zero, then it's a TONE command, and instead of setting the pitch, we set the tone of that channel.

Both channels share the same logical array for tracks and patterns, so both tracks can take up to 255 bytes total, and all patterns can use up to 255 bytes total.

The music player as-implemented uses 8 bytes of RAM (not counting stack). We store the current byte offset into the tracks array, one for each track. Same thing for the patterns array. We also store the current note and duration remaining for each track.

```
trk0idx        equ     $e0     ; offset into tracks for
    channel 0
trk1idx        equ     $e1     ; offset into tracks for
    channel 1
pat0idx        equ     $e2     ; offset into patterns for
    channel 0
pat1idx        equ     $e3     ; offset into patterns for
    channel 1
chan0dur       equ     $e4     ; current note duration
    channel 0
chan1dur       equ     $e5     ; current note duration
    channel 1
chan0note      equ     $e6     ; current note pitch channel 0
chan1note      equ     $e7     ; current note pitch channel 1
```

In our main frame loop, we call the music subroutine during the VBLANK period, once for each channel/track:

```
TIMER_SETUP 37
ldx #0
jsr MusicFrame
ldx #1
```

```
        jsr MusicFrame
        TIMER_WAIT
```

This should take no more than a few scanlines to complete in the worst case. The MusicFrame routine first decrements the note's duration, checking to see if it is finished playing:

```
MusicFrame
        dec chan0dur,x          ; decrement note duration
        bpl SkipLoadNote        ; only load if duration < 0
```

If a note is currently playing, we grab its pitch and set the appropriate TIA register. We also calculate the volume as (*duration_remaining*/2) and stuff that into the TIA volume register:

```
PlayNote
        lda chan0note,x
        sta AUDF0,x
        lda chan0dur,x
        clc
        ror
        sta AUDV0,x
        rts
```

But if there is no note yet playing, or if we just finished one, we have to load the next note in the pattern:

```
TryAgain
        ldy pat0idx,x           ; load index into pattern table
        lda Patterns,y          ; load pattern code
        beq NextPattern         ; end of pattern?
```

If the byte loaded is zero, our pattern has ended and we have to go to NextPattern which loads the next pattern in the track. Otherwise, we continue:

```
        inc pat0idx,x           ; increment pattern index for
    next time
        pha                     ; save A for later
        clc                     ; clear carry for ROR
        ror                     ; shift A right by 5 to get
    top 3 bits
```

175

```
ror
ror
ror
ror
and  #7                          ; only take top 3 bits
beq  NoteTone
```

Note that instead of 5 RORs we could also do 4 ROLs, sinced the rotate instructions shift through the carry bit and wrap around to the other side.

This decodes the note's duration, by shifting right five bits with ROR and isolating the first three bits with AND. We use BEQ to check if the duration is zero, since this indicates a special case with a TONE command. Otherwise, we continue:

```
tay                              ; Y = duration
lda  DurFrames,y                 ; look up in duration table
sta  chan0dur,x                  ; save note duration
pla                              ; pop saved value into A
and  #$1f                        ; extract first 5 bits
sta  chan0note,x                 ; store as note value
```

We've looked up the duration in DurFrames, which gives us the number of frames to play the note. We store that value and then PLA to get the original note so we can extract the first 5 bits as the note's pitch. Then we store that value too, and continue on to PlayNote.

If we had got a TONE command, we'd have a zero duration, and we'd branch to this routine which would set the tone register:

```
NoteTone
        pla
        and  #$f
        beq  NextPattern
        sta  AUDC0,x
        jmp  TryAgain
```

But if we got a TONE 0 command, we'd instead go to NextPattern, which would load the next pattern offset in the track and then continue:

```
NextPattern
        ldy trk0idx,x
        lda Track0,y
        beq ResetTrack
        sta pat0idx,x
        inc trk0idx,x
```

And if the next pattern offset was also zero, we'd reset both tracks back to the beginning:

```
ResetTrack
        lda #0
        sta trk0idx
        lda #Track1-Track0
        sta trk1idx
```

Improvements:

- The NoteTone subroutine just tapers off the volume linearly. We could have a different "envelope" that tapers upwards then downwards, or any other shape driven by a table.

33

Pseudo-3D: Sunsets and Starry Nights

If there's one thing the VCS can't do well, it's 3D graphics! In 1977, the closest thing to a 3D game was Atari's *Night Driver*, which featured a track of black and white rectangular pylons. Nevertheless, game developers quickly learned how to "fake it," giving players the impression of 3D graphics using 2D techniques. This is often refered to as *pseudo-3D*, or "2 1/2-D." It's more art than science, using smoke and mirrors (color and shape) to fool the eye into perceiving depth.

We'll do this scene in multiple segments:

1. Sky, clouds, and sunset
2. Mountains
3. Stars at night

33.1   Sky, Clouds, and Sunset

One easy way to convince the player that they're gazing into the distance is to show them a pretty sunset. The team at Activision specialized in sunsets, starting with the title *Barnstorming*. A sunset-colored stripe even became part of their logo.

It turns out the VCS is pretty good at sunsets, since it has 128 different colors and can draw horizontal lines pretty well.

Figure 33.1: Sunset with clouds and mountains

A convincing sunset is going to need a couple of things. First, it needs to appear to recede to the horizon. So we're going to draw horizontal segments of color starting at 16 pixels of height, then 14, 12, 10, 8, 6, 4, and 2 pixels high.

The sunset is also going to need convincing color. We're going to give each successive segment a different color, looking them up from a table. The table will go from the black of night all the way through the colors of the sunrise and morning to blue, then back again through sunset, twilight, and back to black. Our starting index will be based on time-of-day in the game, so as we cycle around the array, we'll see sunrise and sunset.

We'll also add clouds. We'll just use the playfield registers to display them, and the bitmaps will come from another table. Their color will come from the same table used for the sky color; we'll just offset the index by 2.

This will give the clouds a nice glowing effect at sunrise, since they'll be a little brighter than the sky and give a nice contrast. At sunset, they'll be a little darker. (Fun fact: The cloud tables are actually too short, and the lookups spill over into neighboring arrays, but it looks okay anyway... Rule #1 of VCS programming: if it looks alright, keep it!)

```
        lda TimeOfDay+1 ; offset into sunset color table
        and #$3f
        tay
        lda #16         ; initial height of sky segment
.SkyLoop2
        tax             ; height -> X
        pha             ; push original height
.SkyLoop
        lda SunsetColors,y      ; get sunset color
        sta WSYNC              ; start scanline
```

```
      sta COLUBK              ; set background color
      lda SunsetColors+2,y    ; get cloud color
      sta COLUPF              ; set foreground color
      lda CloudPFData0,x      ; load clouds -> playfield
      sta PF0
      lda CloudPFData1,x
      sta PF1
      lda CloudPFData2,x
      sta PF2
      dex
      bne .SkyLoop            ; repeat until sky segment done
      iny                     ; next sky color
      tya
      and #$3f                ; keep sky color in range 0-63
      tay                     ; sky color -> Y
      pla                     ; restore original segment
height
      sec
      sbc #2                  ; segment height - 2
      cmp #2                  ; done with segments?
      bcs .SkyLoop2           ; no, repeat
```

33.2 Mountains

Now, after the sky is done, we'll draw a short seven-line segment of mountains. This will give an even more interesting look. We'll again use the playfield for the mountains, and make them a flat color. We'll keep incrementing the sky color on every scanline to make the sunset look like it's peeking out from behind the mountains.

We'll also have the mountains change colors during the game-day, using a lookup table with only 16 entries (as opposed to 64 for the sky and clouds). This is similar to the previous loop, except we do one scanline at a time. We also have a 16-entry table for the ground color, which we'll set after we draw the mountains.

```
      lda TimeOfDay+1
      lsr
      lsr                     ; divide time-of-day by 4
      and #$f                 ; keep in range 0-15
      tax                     ; -> Y
```

181

```
            lda  MountainColors,x     ; load mountain color
            sta  COLUPF               ; set foreground
            lda  GroundColors,x       ; load ground color
            pha                       ; save it for later
            ldx  #0
            stx  PF0
            stx  PF1                  ; to avoid artifacts, we have
     to
            stx  PF2                  ; clear previous clouds
.MtnLoop
            lda  SunsetColors,y       ; get sunset color
            sta  WSYNC                ; start scanline
            sta  COLUBK               ; set background color
            lda  MtnPFData0,x         ; load mountains -> playfield
            sta  PF0
            lda  MtnPFData1,x
            sta  PF1
            lda  MtnPFData2,x
            sta  PF2
            iny                       ; next sky color
            tya
            and  #$3f                 ; keep sky color in range 0-63
            tay                       ; sky color -> Y
            inx
            cpx  #7                   ; only 7 scanlines for the
     mountains
            bne  .MtnLoop
            pla                  ; restore ground color
            sta  COLUBK          ; set background
```

33.3 Stars at Night

Since drawing the sky is fun, let's try to do a night sky with stars. This takes advantage of a TIA "feature" involving the ball object. Whenever you reset the ball position with RESBL, the TIA draws it immediately at the current TIA color clock. You can draw as many balls as you want on a given scanline, and if you strobe RESBL in a loop across multiple scanlines, you can make a pattern of dots.

For stars, we're going to wait a "random" time between each ball. We don't need a lot of variation, but just enough to make sure the stars don't line up in any discernable pattern. So we

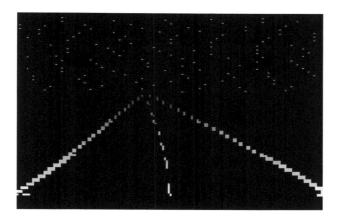

Figure 33.2: Pseudo-3d road with stars

generate pseudorandom numbers by reading the code in ROM, test/shift a few of their bits, and use branch instructions (which take three cycles if the branch is taken, two if not) to add between zero and four additional cycles between each star. This gives us a nice star density but also adds enough spacing that the stars look randomly distributed.

To figure out when to stop drawing stars, we'll read the timer register and stop when it goes below a predetermined value.

```
DrawNight subroutine
        lda #6
        sta ENABL        ; enable ball
        sta COLUPF       ; set ball color
        ldy #0
.MoreStars
        sta RESBL        ; strobe the ball to display a star
        adc Start,y      ; "randomize" the A register
        bmi .Delay1      ; +1 cycle if bit 7 set
.Delay1
        ror              ; shift lo bit into carry
        bcs .Delay2      ; +1 cycle if bit 0 set
.Delay2
        ror              ; shift lo bit into carry
        bcs .Delay3      ; +1 cycle if bit 1 set
.Delay3
        ror              ; shift lo bit into carry
        bcs .Delay4      ; +1 cycle if bit 2 set
```

```
.Delay4
        iny                 ; next "random" number
        ldx INTIM           ; load timer
        cpx #$89            ; timer says we're done?
        bcs .MoreStars      ; nope, make more stars
        lda #0
        sta ENABL           ; disable ball
        rts
```

You can tweak the various delay branches until you get a star pattern that looks good to you.

So far so good; we've got a nice little gradiated sky with clouds and mountains, and a solid-colored ground. In the next chapter we'll learn how to build a curving road disappearing to the horizon.

> **TIP:** To see this code and the code from Chapter 34: Driving Down the Road in action and directly manipulate it in real-time, check out the Pseudo 3D example on 8bitworkshop.com.

34

Pseudo-3D: Driving Down the Road

You may have seen games on the VCS like Activision's *Enduro* and Atari's *Pole Position* that are from the perspective of a camera above and behind a car. The car is driving on a track that disappears into the horizon. It's not sorcery, just some clever manipulation of TIA graphics objects.

We already used the playfield to draw clouds and mountains, but we're going to now leave that alone and use the two missiles and ball objects. With these, we'll draw the two shoulders of the road, and also the dashed center line.

Our plan is this: The two missiles and ball all start at the same position on the horizon. As we go down the screen, we'll move the three objects slightly based on the curve of the road. The left shoulder of the road will be biased a little more to the left, and the right shoulder will bias a little more right. We can use the HMOVE registers for movement, since each object will not need to move more than seven pixels on any given scanline.

It'd be easier if the scanlines went from bottom to top, because we could just start at the horizontal center of the screen and follow the road curve to the horizon, ending up wherever the road takes us. But scanlines go top to bottom, so we have to also do some preprocessing before the frame begins to figure out where the road ends up.

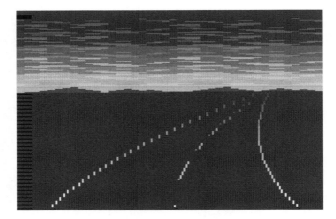

Figure 34.1: Pseudo-3d road with sunset

We're also going to need an array to define the contours of the track as it ascends to the horizon. We'll generate this curve data on-demand using the random number generators described in previous chapters. Positive values indicate a curve to the right, negative values curve left.

So let's review our plan:

1. **Preprocessing:** Evaluate the track from near-to-far, building an array of X coordinates from bottom-to-horizon.
2. **Setup:** Set all three objects (missile 0, missile 1, ball) to the same X position, which is the final point we just evaluated closest to the horizon.
3. **Kernel:** Draw successive road segments from far to near, moving the three objects in accord with the X coordinate array we built. To show perspective, we'll bias missile 0 to the left and missile 1 to the right. The ball will be used to draw the centerline.
4. **Generate:** Add the player's speed to the fractional track position, and if this overflows, generate a new piece of track curve data.

Each of these steps will be a little complicated, so we'll go one at a time. First, we'll describe the preprocessing step.

Because we want our track to be able to curve by less than one pixel, we'll use fixed-point math (as described in Chapter 31).

We'll use a 16-bit value for the current X coordinate, and a 16-bit value for the current line slope (XVel).

We start at the bottom center of the screen, and, as we evaluate the curve into the distance, we modify XPos (horizontal position) using XVel (horizontal slope), and modify TPos (the track position) using TrackLookahead (the increment of the track position at each step).

The C-ish pseudocode looks like this:

```
XPos = 72;
TPos = TrackFrac;
for (int i=31; i>=0; i++) {
        XPos += XVel;
        RoadX[i] = XPos>>8;
        XVel += TrackData[TPos>>8];
        TPos += TrackLookahead;
        TrackLookahead++;
}
```

We only need an 8-bit value for TrackFrac, which is the *fractional track position*: how far the player has traveled along the track. If we were keeping the curve data for the track in ROM, we'd use a 16-bit value and use the high byte to index into that array. But since we generate track data on-demand, we shift the array and only use the fractional part of the track position.

Note that the 6502 does not have a "shift right 8 bits" instruction – how could it, with 8-bit registers? Instead, we just load the high byte of the 16-bit number. For example, LDA XPos loads the low byte, and LDA XPos+1 loads the high byte.

Here's the code:

```
XPos              .word   ; 16-bit X position
XVel              .word   ; 16-bit X velocity
TPos              .word   ; 16-bit track position
TrackLookahead    .byte   ; current fractional track increment

NumRoadSegments equ 28
; Preprocessing result: X positions for all track segments
RoadX0                    REPEAT NumRoadSegments
                          .byte
```

```
                      REPEND

; Setup initial values
        lda #0
        sta XVel
        sta XVel+1
        sta XPos
        lda #70          ; approx. center of screen
        sta XPos+1
        lda TrackFrac
        sta TPos
        lda #0
        sta TPos+1
        lda #10          ; initial lookahead
        sta TrackLookahead
        ldx #NumRoadSegments-1

.CurveLoop
; Modify X position
; XPos += XVel (16 bit add)
        lda XPos
        clc
        adc XVel
        sta XPos
        lda XPos+1
        adc XVel+1
        sta XPos+1
        sta RoadX0,x     ; store in RoadX0 array
; Modify X velocity (slope)
; XVel += TrackData[TPos]
        ldy TPos+1       ; get track data offset
        lda TrackData,y  ; load track curve data
        clc              ; clear carry for ADC
        bmi .CurveLeft   ; track slope negative?
        adc XVel
        sta XVel
        lda XVel+1
        adc #0           ; carry +1
        jmp .NoCurveLeft
.CurveLeft
        adc XVel
        sta XVel
        lda XVel+1
        sbc #0           ; carry -1
        nop ; make the branch timings are the same
.NoCurveLeft
        sta XVel+1
```

```
; Advance TPos (TrackData index)
; TPos += TrackLookahead
        lda TPos
        clc
        adc TrackLookahead
        sta TPos
        lda TPos+1
        adc #0
        sta TPos+1
; Go to next segment
        inc TrackLookahead ; see further along track
        dex
        bpl .CurveLoop
```

The preprocessing routine takes up a fair number of cycles; in fact we can't really do it in the standard 37-line VBLANK section, so we extend VBLANK to 40 lines.

Now we have to set up the TIA moveable objects. We load the first X coordinate of our array, which is the last coordinate we computed and the one closest to the horizon. Then we use the tried-and-true SetHorizPos technique to set the position of the two missiles and ball, all in the same scanline. We'll use a lookup table (HMoveTable) to save a couple of cycles.

```
            lda RoadX0      ; get horizon X position
            sta HMCLR       ; clear HMOVE registers
            sec             ; set carry for SBC
            sta WSYNC
.DivideLoop
            sbc #15         ; subtract 15
            bcs .DivideLoop ; branch while carry still set
            adc #15         ; +15 to make positive remainder
            tay
            lda HMoveTable,y ; lookup HMOVE value
            sta HMM0        ; set missile 0 fine offset
            sta HMBL        ; set ball fine offset
            sta HMM1        ; set missile 1 fine offset
            sta RESM0       ; set missile 0 position
            sta RESBL       ; set ball position
            sta RESM1       ; set missile 1 position
            sta WSYNC
            sta HMOVE       ; apply fine offsets
```

Because the three STA RESM0/RESBL/RESM1 instructions take three cycles each, our objects will be nine pixels apart. We'd like them a little closer than that, so we do an HMOVE for each of them to bring them a little closer together:

```
lda #$90        ; right 7 pixels
ldy #$70        ; left 7 pixels
ldx #$00        ; no movement
sta HMM0
sty HMM1
stx HMBL
sta WSYNC
sta HMOVE       ; apply fine offsets
```

> Historical Note: *Pole Position* used the BRK instruction to set all three HMxx registers in just three cycles – I'll leave it as an exercise to the reader to figure out how they did it!

You might be wondering why we load all three registers before storing all three values – it's because the HMxx registers don't like being set within 24 CPU cycles of strobing HMOVE, or weird things can happen. So we give them a little breathing room.

Now that we have our moveable objects where we want them at the horizon, we walk back up the road (down the screen). For each segment, we look up the X coordinate difference between this segment and the next. Then we look up the appropriate value in HMoveTable to move the center line object (the ball). For the left and right shoulders, we simply look up a value in HMoveTable offset by -2 or +2 so that each side is biased toward the left or right:

```
        lda TrackFrac
        asl
        asl             ; TrackFrac * 4
        sta Z0fs        ; for animated stripe
        ldx #0
.RoadLoop
        lda RoadColors,x ; color of sides and center line
        sta COLUP0
```

```
sta COLUP1
sta COLUPF
lda RoadX0+1,x   ; get next X coordinate
sec
sbc RoadX0,x     ; subtract this X coordinate
clc
adc #7           ; add 7
tay              ; -> Y
lda HMoveTable-2,y       ; left side biased -2
sta HMM0                 ; -> missile 0 fine offset
lda HMoveTable,y         ; center line
sta HMBL                 ; -> ball fine offset
lda HMoveTable+2,y       ; right side biased +2
sta HMM1                 ; -> missile 1 fine offset
sta WSYNC
sta HMOVE                ; apply fine offsets
sta WSYNC
```

The dashed road stripe is a prime example of "fake it 'til you make it" and its appearance has nothing to do with geometry. We initialize a counter to the fractional track position, then we subtract the PIA timer (which decreases as we go down the screen) for each segment as an approximation of Z distance (the Z coordinate = into the screen).

We also have a lookup table that we use to load the NUSIZ registers so that the missiles (road shoulders) get wider as we get closer to the bottom of the screen:

```
lda Z0fs
sec
sbc INTIM
sta Z0fs         ; Z0fs -= timer
rol
rol
rol              ; shift left by 3
sta ENABL        ; enable ball (bit 2)
sta WSYNC
lda RoadWidths,x ; lookup register for missile size
sta NUSIZ0
sta NUSIZ1
sta WSYNC
inx
cpx #NumRoadSegments-1
bne .RoadLoop
```

Finally, we describe how we generate the track curve data. The curve data is stored in a five-byte buffer – this is about as far as our display routines look ahead. When a new value needs to be generated, we'll discard the first (nearest to the camera) value, move the other values up one slot, and put the new value in the last (furthest toward the horizon) slot. We'll do this whenever the TrackFrac value overflows, and the player won't even notice the transition.

To make meandering curves, we'll have a target value (GenTarget), a current value (GenCur), and a delta value (GenDelta). We'll move the current value toward the target, and whenever they cross we'll make a new random target and delta value, ensuring that the delta value is always going in the direction of the target. The pseudocode looks like this:

```
PrevGenCur = GenCur
GenCur += GenDelta
if ((GenCur >= GenTarget && GenTarget >= 0) ||
    (GenCur < GenTarget && GenTarget < 0)) {
        GenTarget = random number from -31..32
        if (GenTarget - GenCur >= 0)
                GenDelta = random number from 1..15
        else
                GenDelta = random number from -15..-1
        GenCur = PrevGenCur
}
```

Here's the code:

```
Random          .byte    ; random counter
GenTarget       .byte    ; target of current curve
GenDelta        .byte    ; curve delta
GenCur          .byte    ; current curve value

; Generated track curve data
TrackLen        equ 5
TrackData       REPEAT TrackLen
                .byte
                REPEND

GenTrack subroutine
; Shift the existing track data one byte up
; (a[i] = a[i+1])
```

```
        ldx #0
.ShiftTrackLoop
        lda TrackData+1,x
        sta TrackData,x
        inx
        cpx #TrackLen-1
        bne .ShiftTrackLoop
; Modify our current track value and
; see if it intersects the target value
        lda GenCur
        clc
        adc GenDelta
        cmp GenTarget
        beq .ChangeTarget   ; target == cur?
        bit GenTarget       ; see if target >=0 or <0
        bmi .TargetNeg
        bcs .ChangeTarget   ; target>=0 && cur>=target
        bcc .NoChangeTarget
.TargetNeg
        bcs .NoChangeTarget ; target<0 && cur<target
; Generate a new target value and increment value,
; and make sure the increment value is positive if
; the target is above the current value, and negative
; otherwise
.ChangeTarget
        jsr NextRandom ; get a random value
        and #$3f        ; range 0..63
        sec
        sbc #$1f        ; range -31..32
        sta GenTarget   ; -> target
        cmp GenCur
        bmi .TargetBelow ; current > target?
        jsr NextRandom ; get a random value
        and #$f         ; mask to 0..15
        jmp .TargetAbove
.TargetBelow
        jsr NextRandom
        ora #$f0        ; mask to -16..0
.TargetAbove
        ora #1          ; to avoid 0 values
        sta GenDelta    ; -> delta
        lda GenCur
.NoChangeTarget
; Store the value in GenCur, and also
; at the end of the TrackData array
        sta GenCur
        sta TrackData+TrackLen-1
```

```
rts
```

> **TIP:** To see this code in action and directly manipulate it in real-time, check out the Pseudo 3D example on 8bitworkshop.com.

There are several improvements we could make to this:

- We only move the road objects every four scanlines. This makes road shoulders in the distance look like tall pylons. It'd be better if we could move every scanline, but we don't have enough memory or CPU cycles to compute and store 112 lines of X positions. One possible solution is to use multiple HMOVE lookup tables to interpolate each TIA object between two X positions.
- We could add sprites of several different scales to represent cars and road objects. We could probably use the same HMOVE technique to move them, as long as we limit ourselves to two sprites per screen. Alternatively, we could sneak in a repositioning step on a spare scanline. One problem is that we've already set all three of our color registers to the same value, so we'd either have to make sprites the same color or lose the center line.
- There are lots of different ways to color the road graphics – alternating stripe colors, or schemes that depend on changing weather.
- Allow the viewpoint to move left and right between lanes. Since you want to keep the vanishing point at the horizon fixed, you'd have to introduce a bias to the preprocessing step that's proportional to the offset of the viewpoint.
- Implement clipping, where we'd track the position of the road components and hide them when they stray off the sides of the screen.
- Can we draw a sun? A moon? A speedometer? A track timer?

35

Bank Switching

The VCS design has a couple of significant limitations that we've discussed:

- 128 bytes of RAM
- 4096 (4KB) of ROM program memory

Thanks to a "forgiving" architecture, many games have gotten around both limitations by adding hardware to the cartridge itself. For example, the *Super Chip* was an extension from Atari that added another 128 bytes of RAM, which was usually mapped at address $1000. Only later games like *Dig Dug* and *Crystal Castles* took advantage of this.

The ROM limitation was a bit trickier. The VCS has a cheaper variant of the 6502 (the 6507) that is physically missing address bus pins, and so can only map 8KB of memory. 4KB of that is reserved for cartridge ROM, and there's no way for the cartridge to expose anything beyond its address space at $1000-1FFF.

Because of the missing pins of the 6507, the full 16-bit address space is not used, and only 13 bits are valid. Since we can only address 2^{13} ($2000) bytes, the following ranges are equivalent:

```
$0000-$1FFF, $2000-$3FFF, $4000-$5FFF, $6000-$7FFF
$8000-$9FFF, $A000-$BFFF, $C000-$DFFF, $E000-$FFFF
```

By convention, most people use $F000-$FFFF for non-bankswitched 4K ROMs.

Starting with the Atari port of *Asteroids*, many cartridges got around the 4KB ROM code limit using a method called *bankswitching*. The cartridge uses the same 4KB address space, but can swap in different sections of code when the CPU touches a special set of *soft switch* addresses in ROM address space.

There are many different bankswitching methods, and they're commonly referred to by the address of the first soft switch. We'll talk about F8 bankswitching, which is the earliest method.

F8 bankswitching has two soft switchs, $1FF8 and $1FF9. Accessing the first address switches to bank #0, accessing the second switches to bank #1. Each bank is 4KB, so the entire 4K region from $1000-$1FFF is replaced.

The bank switch happens more or less instantaneously as far as the CPU is concerned. What happens if the CPU is currently executing instructions in the section being swapped out? The PC (Program Counter) remains the same, but the next instruction fetched will be from the new ROM segment. If we're not careful, we could switch out the current instruction from under our feet!

35.1 Trampolines

One way to be safe is to put a *trampoline* at the same location in all ROM segments to safely switch banks without the rug being pulled out under you. Instead, we *bounce* into another code bank. The trampoline needs to hit the soft switch address, then transfer control to a new routine. We might use the trampoline like so:

```
ldy #<(NewRoutine-1)    ; lo byte of new PC
lda #>(NewRoutine-1)    ; hi byte of new PC
ldx #0                  ; bank number
jmp BankSwitch          ; do the switch
```

The trampoline would look like this:

```
BankSwitch
        pha             ; push hi byte
        tya             ; Y -> A
        pha             ; push lo byte
        bit $1FF8,x     ; do the bank switch
        rts             ; return to target
```

This is a pretty succinct trampoline, but requires some explaining. We're using the RTS instruction to transfer control to a new location after the bank switch, but without a JSR. Instead, we're faking the JSR by pushing the return address of the non-existent JSR onto the stack, which we've passed in registers Y and A to the trampoline. When we RTS, the CPU will pop off the address and go where we want.

Note that we use the address (NewRoutine-1) as the destination – this is because RTS increments the Program Counter before executing the next instruction. Make sure you use the parenthesis, because you want to subtract before taking the lo/hi byte, not afterwards.

There's another case we need to worry about, which is power-up time. We don't know which bank will be selected at power-up, so the first thing we need to do is select it and jump to the starting routine. The easiest way is to just put this code right before the trampoline:

```
BankResetStart
        ldy #<(Start-1)
        lda #>(Start-1)
        ldx #0
        ; ... execution continues with trampoline
```

Then we just ensure that each bank contains an identical RESET vector in $FFFC/FFFD that points to this routine, and that the BankResetStart/BankSwitch code is present at the same location in all banks.

In a real program, you'd probably use a macro to make this stuff foolproof. The example in subsection 35.4 demonstrates this.

You can also check out the Bankswitching example available in the 8bitworkshop emulator.

NOTE: When bankswitching, we always use a read instruction (BIT and CMP work well, or even the undocumented nop aaaa instruction) because write instructions may cause bus conflicts.

35.2 Common Bankswitching Methods

There are three "simple" bankswitching schemes used in Atari games:

Method	Size	Soft Switches
F8	8K	$1FF8-$1FF9
F6	16K	$1FF6-$1FF9
F4	32K	$1FF4-$1FFB

Table 35.1: Common Bankswitching Schemes

There are many other third-party and homebrew mapping schemes; you can find more detailed descriptions online[7].

35.3 ORG vs. RORG

You might see statements in bankswitched code that look like this:

```
;;; BANK 0
        org $1000
        rorg $F000
;;; BANK 1
        org $2000
        rorg $F000
```

We've seen ORG before, but not RORG. ORG means *origin* and RORG means *relocatable origin*. ORG affects where the code is physically placed in the ROM image, but RORG is where the code *thinks* it's placed. In most VCS bankswitching methods, the ORGs will be evenly spaced and the RORGs will be identical.

35.4 Bankswitching Example

```
        processor 6502
        include "vcs.h"
        include "macro.h"
        include "xmacro.h"

;;;;;;;;;;;;;;;;;;;;;;;;;;;;;;;;;;;;;;;;;;;;;;;;;;;;;;;;;;;;;;

        seg.u Variables
        org $80

Temp    .byte

;;;;;;;;;;;;;;;;;;;;;;;;;;;;;;;;;;;;;;;;;;;;;;;;;;;;;;;;;;;;;;

; Macro that implements Bank Switching trampoline
; X = bank number
; A = hi byte of destination PC
; Y = lo byte of destination PC
        MAC BANK_SWITCH_TRAMPOLINE
        pha                 ; push hi byte
        tya                 ; Y -> A
        pha                 ; push lo byte
        lda $1FF8,x         ; do the bank switch
        rts                 ; return to target
        ENDM

; Macro that performs bank switch
        MAC BANK_SWITCH
.Bank   SET {1}
.Addr   SET {2}
        lda #>(.Addr-1)
        ldy #<(.Addr-1)
        ldx #.Bank
        jmp BankSwitch
        ENDM

        seg Code
;;;;;;;;;;;;;;;;;;;;;;;;;;;;;;;;;;;;;;;;;;;;;;;;;;;;;;;;;;;;;;
;;; BANK 0

        org $1000
        rorg $F000
;----The following code is the same on both banks----
Start
```

```
; Ensure that bank 0 is selected
        lda #>(Reset_0-1)
        ldy #<(Reset_0-1)
        ldx #0
BankSwitch
        BANK_SWITCH_TRAMPOLINE
;----End of bank-identical code----
Reset_0
        CLEAN_START
        lda #$30
        sta COLUBK        ; make the screen red
        bit INPT4         ; test button
        bmi Reset_0       ; button not pressed, repeat
; Switch to Bank 2 routine
        lda #>(Main_1-1)
        ldy #<(Main_1-1)
        ldx #1
        jmp BankSwitch

; Bank 0 epilogue
        org $1FFA
        rorg $FFFA
        .word Start       ; NMI
        .word Start       ; RESET
        .word Start       ; BRK


;;;;;;;;;;;;;;;;;;;;;;;;;;;;;;;;;;;;;;;;;;;;;;;;;;;;;;;;;;;;;;;;
;;; BANK 1

        org $2000
        rorg $F000
;----The following code is the same on both banks----
Start
; Ensure that bank 0 is selected
        lda #>(Reset_0-1)
        ldy #<(Reset_0-1)
        ldx #0
BankSwitch
        BANK_SWITCH_TRAMPOLINE
;----End of bank-identical code----
Main_1
        inc Temp
        lda Temp
        sta COLUBK        ; make rainbows
        bit INPT4         ; test button
        bpl Main_1        ; button is pressed, repeat
        BANK_SWITCH 0,Reset_0
```

```
; Bank 1 epilogue
        org $2FFA
        rorg $FFFA
        .word Start        ; NMI
        .word Start        ; RESET
        .word Start        ; BRK
```

36

Wavetable Audio

The VCS can produce a variety of shrill and flatulent noises which work surprisingly well for sound effects, but unless you're a fan of "flat twos" and the Phrygian mode, you may not be completely satisfied with its musical abilities.

Activision's *Pitfall 2* was the zenith of VCS technical achievements in 1984. It featured a custom "Display Processor Chip" (DPC) chip inside the cartridge, to which the CPU would offload several CPU-intensive functions like sprite calculation. Another thing it would do is generate three-voice music and pipe it through a single VCS sound channel.

It turns out we can do the same thing the DPC chip does with music, except we'll use most of our CPU time doing it.

36.1   Audio Waveforms

A digital device produces audio by varying the amplitude of a waveform at fixed intervals, driven by a table of values. Each value is called a *sample*. On the VCS, these samples are all generated by the TIA chip output at configurable frequencies.

Instead of letting the TIA have all the fun, we can have the CPU output samples. The TIA has a mode (0) that continuously outputs a flat signal. If the CPU varies the volume of the TIA's output, it can generate its own waveform.

For timing, we can use the TIA's scanline generator. It outputs 262 scanlines per frame, 60 times a second, which gives us an effective upper frequency of 15720 Hz. The range of human hearing is usually 10-17 Khz, so this will be fine.

36.2   Generating Samples

For each software-generated voice, we have a 16-bit cycle counter, and a 16-bit delta value. When we need a sample, we add the delta to the cycle counter and use the high byte to look up a value in the wavetable. Using pseudocode, this looks like:

```
Cycle = (Cycle + Delta) & $1F00
AUDV0 = Wavetable[Hi(Cycle) & $1F]
```

Here's the equivalent 6502 code:

```
        lda Cycle0Lo
        clc
        adc Delta0Lo
        sta Cycle0Lo
        lda Cycle0Hi
        adc Delta0Hi
        and #$1F
        sta Cycle0Hi             ; Cycle = (Cycle+Delta) &
0x1f00
        tay                      ; hi byte -> Y
        lda Wavetable,y          ; lookup sample in wavetable
        sta AUDV0                ; store in audio volume
register
```

To mix two voices together, we just perform this operation twice and average the result:

```
; Get first channel phase, put in X
        lda Cycle0Lo
        clc
        adc Delta0Lo
        sta Cycle0Lo
        lda Cycle0Hi
        adc Delta0Hi
        and #$1F
        sta Cycle0Hi
```

```
        tax
; Get second channel phase, put in Y
        lda Cycle1Lo
        clc
        adc Delta1Lo
        sta Cycle1Lo
        lda Cycle1Hi
        adc Delta1Hi
        and #$1F
        sta Cycle0Hi
        tay
; Lookup wavetable entry and sum
        lda Wavetable,y
        clc
        adc Wavetable,x
; Divide by 2 and store to volume register
        lsr
        sta AUDV0
```

We can mix two voices for each TIA audio channel for a total of four simultaneous voices. This takes the CPU about 140 cycles, which is almost two scanlines, so when generating four-voice wavetable audio, we don't have time left over to do much video, unfortunately. It also gives us an upper frequency of 7860 Hz.

Our wavetable is 32 bytes long. This table defines a simple triangle-shaped wave, but it could be a sine wave or any other form:

```
Wavetable
        hex 00010203 04050607 08090a0b 0c0d0e0f
        hex 0f0e0d0c 0b0a0908 07060504 03020100
```

We can use a precomputed table of delta values for each note in the chromatic scale:

```
        align $100
NoteDeltas
        word 9, 9, 10, 10, 11, 11, 12, 13, 14, 14, 15, 16
        word 17, 18, 19, 20, 22, 23, 24, 26, 27, 29, 30, 32
        word 34, 36, 38, 41, 43, 46, 48, 51, 54, 57, 61, 65
        word 68, 72, 77, 81, 86, 91, 97, 102, 108, 115, 122,
    129
        word 137, 145, 153, 163, 172, 182, 193, 205, 217, 230,
    244, 258
```

```
        word 273, 290, 307, 325, 344, 365, 387, 410, 434, 460,
487, 516
        word 547, 579, 614, 650, 689, 730, 773, 819, 868, 920,
974, 1032
        word 1093, 1159, 1227, 1300, 1378, 1460, 1546, 1638,
1736, 1839, 1948, 2064
        word 2187, 2317, 2455, 2601, 2755, 2919, 3093, 3277,
3472, 3678, 3897, 4128
        word 4374, 4634, 4910, 5202, 5511, 5839, 6186, 6554,
6943, 7356, 7793, 8257
        word 8748, 9268, 9819, 10403, 11022, 11677, 12371,
13107
```

And load them into one of the 4 voices like this:

```
        ldy #48
        lda NoteDeltas,y
        sta Delta0Lo
        lda NoteDeltas+1,y
        sta Delta0Hi
```

All we've done here is play a droning infinite chord, but you could extend this code to make a music player by loading different notes at appropriate intervals, as we do in the Wavetable Sound example in the 8bitworkshop emulator. Displaying graphics at the same time would be tricky to say the least, but dedicated Atari homebrew authors have done it (look for a cartridge called *Stella's Stocking* online).

37

Paddles

The paddles are potentiometers (knobs) that travel 330 degrees and have a single button. The VCS supports up to four of them. There's really no equivalent device on most standard game controllers or keyboards, but here's how to read them anyway.

First, reading the switches on each paddle is just like reading the joysticks/switches, as we did in Chapter 19. There are 4 bits in the SWCHA register, one for each paddle:

Paddle #	Register	Bit #
0	SWCHA	7
1	SWCHA	6
2	SWCHA	3
3	SWCHA	2

Table 37.1: Paddle Buttons

Just like the joysticks, the bit is 0 if the paddle button is pressed, 1 otherwise.

Reading the potentiometer (knob) value is a little more complicated. We would like a single number that reads 0 when the paddle is turned all the way counter-clockwise, and at its maximum (say, 255 or $FF) when turned all the way clockwise. But that's not how it works on the VCS.

The paddles are connected to a capacitor, which charges at different rates depending on the position of the potentiometer.

You read the paddle position by measuring the time it takes for the potentiometer to discharge. Oddly enough, the capacitor is controlled by the VBLANK register:

```
        VERTICAL_SYNC
        lda #$82
        sta VBLANK ; turn off video; dump paddles to ground

        TIMER_SETUP 37
        TIMER_WAIT
        lda #0
        sta VBLANK ; turn on video; remove ground dump
```

The paddles take a while to discharge, so you have to poll (check) the paddle values during the video kernel loop:

```
        TIMER_SETUP 192
.Loop
        lda INTIM       ; get timer value
        beq .Exit
        bit INPT0       ; paddle discharged?
        bpl .Discharged ; yes, store value
        .byte $2c       ; skip next insn (BIT opcode)
.Discharged
        sta Paddle1     ; store paddle value
; ... draw video ...
        jmp .Loop
.Exit
```

Note that this loop doesn't draw anything, it just checks the paddle position continuously until the bottom of the frame. If you wanted to add graphics, you'd have to add STA WSYNCs and other stuff, but keep the paddle-checking code (you could make it a macro, too).

If the paddle is turned all the way right, it will discharge almost immediately. If centered, it will take about 190 scanlines to discharge. It turned all the way left, it will take about 380 scanlines – way more than the number of scanlines in a frame!

This means you not only have to check paddles during the 192 scanlines of your visible frame, but all through the overscan, VSYNC and VBLANK periods too – and measuring a single

Hex Addr	Name	Bits Used 76543210	Description
38	INPT0	x.......	Dumped Input Port 0
39	INPT1	x.......	Dumped Input Port 1
3A	INPT2	x.......	Dumped Input Port 2
3B	INPT3	x.......	Dumped Input Port 3

Table 37.2: Paddle Registers

paddle might take two frames! This is highly annoying, which explains why most VCS games used the joysticks.

Confused by this code?

```
10 01           bpl .Discharged ; yes, store value
2c              .byte $2c       ; skip next insn (BIT)
        .Discharged
85 80           sta Paddle1     ; store paddle value
```

When the branch is taken, the STA instruction executes. When it isn't taken, the $2C opcode is interpreted as a BIT aaaa instruction, and the two bytes of the STA instruction are interpreted as its operand – in other words, the STA is not executed.

Another handy property of this routine is that no matter which branch is taken, the timing will be the same (6 cycles).

38

Illegal Opcodes

Translating the 8-bit opcode for a 6502 instruction into actions that the CPU can perform is called *decoding*, and it requires a fair bit of silicon to pull off. Not every opcode is a valid instruction – some instructions are considered "illegal," and the chip designers decided to save silicon by not explicitly preventing them from executing.

Most of these illegal instructions don't crash the CPU, but result in odd combinations of other instructions – if this was David Letterman, they might be on the segment "Stupid CPU Tricks!"

However, some of them can be useful in some situations. It's unlikely that early VCS developers took advantage of them, because they were probably worried about compatibility with future hardware. But if you are willing to break the official rules, you can save a few cycles where there's no other good option. (Note that some recent Atari clones, like the Flashback 2, are reported not to support these instructions, so *caveat emptor*.)

A lot of these instructions combine two different 6502 operations, for instance:

SAX - Performs a bitwise AND with A and X, then stores the result. No flags are affected.
LAX - LDA then TAX. All addressing modes are available except for immediate.

ANC - AND with immediate mode operand then copy bit 7 (Negative/Sign) to Carry.

ASR - AND with immediate mode operand then LSR.

ARR - AND then ROR. Sets Carry and Overflow bits strangely.

SBX - X = (A AND X)-#operand. Sets Negative, Zero, Carry.

Some of these instructions read memory, modify the result, and then write back to memory.

DCP - DEC followed by CMP.

ISB - INC followed by SBC.

RLA - ROL followed by AND.

RRA - ROR followed by ADC.

SLO - ASL followed by ORA.

SRE - LSR followed by EOR.

The DCP instruction is handy for sprite-drawing routines, because you often have to decrement a line-counter variable and then compare it to a sprite-height variable. For example:

```
lda #SpriteHeight
dcp LinesLeft
bcs SkipDraw
```

The ISB instruction can be used similarly, which we saw in Chapter 16.

Precise Pitch via Duty Cycling

We learned how to play music on the VCS in Chapter 32. Since each of the two sound channels can generate 96 possible frequencies (32 for each of the 3 base clocks), many notes were out of tune. If we're willing to spend a little more CPU time, we can get more accurate pitch.

We accomplish this by *duty cycling* (or *modulating*) the frequency divisor for each channel. In other words, we switch between two adjacent frequency values, potentially lingering on one value longer than the other. If this is done rapidly, the human ear perceives the average frequency.

For example, if we emit a 400 Hz tone 75% of the time, and a 440 Hz tone 25% of the time, the average frequency perceived will be $(400 * 0.75 + 440 * 0.25) = 410$ Hz.

Our new music player will have three different lookup tables to lookup the AUDC, AUDF, and duty cycle for each note. The duty cycle is given in a bitmask:

```
; Table of AUDC values for each note
TONEZ    .byte 0, 0, 0, 0, 6, 6, 6, 6, 6, 6, 6, 6, 6, 6, ...

; Table of AUDF base values for each note
FREQZ    .byte 30, 30, 30, 30, 30, 28, 26, 25, 23, 22, 21 ...

; Table of duty-cycle bits for each note
DUTYZ    .byte 247, 247, 247, 247, 1, 73, 219, 1, 219, 73 ...
```

For our new music player, we'll allow each channel to switch frequencies eight times per frame, or 480 Hz. (This could be reduced to 1 or 2 times per frame, but "vibrato" would be more apparent.) Every 2 msec, we rotate the bitmask and add the next bit to the divisor – cycling between two neighboring divisors.

We'll write two macros to make our main loop simpler. DUTYCYCLE is expanded six times per frame, and calls the DutyCycle subroutine to rotate the duty cycle bitmask and update the AUDFx register for each channel. It also calls DrawBitmap which renders playfield lines until the timer register (INTIM) goes below 2:

```
MAC DUTYCYCLE
TIMER_SETUP 34
jsr DutyCycle    ; cycle notes
jsr DrawBitmap   ; draw ~33 lines of bitmap
ENDM
```

The PULSE macro is expanded twice per frame, and does the same thing as DUTYCYCLE except it also decrements the volumes for each channel and the note timer, fetching the next note if neccessary:

```
MAC PULSE
TIMER_SETUP 35
jsr DutyCycle    ; cycle notes
jsr Pulse        ; decrement duration timer
jsr DrawBitmap   ; draw ~34 lines of bitmap
ENDM
```

The Pulse subroutine may take a couple extra scanlines to execute if it has to fetch the next note from the song data. Since we use the timer to figure out when to stop drawing the bitmap, we'll never use too many scanlines, though our bitmap may "jump" when notes are fetched (we could fix this with a little more care.)

So here's our main kernel loop, run once per frame:

```
NextFrame
        VERTICAL_SYNC   ; 4 scanlines
        lda #$d0
        sta BitmapY     ; reset to top of bitmap
```

```
PULSE                 ; 34 scanlines
DUTYCYCLE             ; 32 scanlines
DUTYCYCLE             ; 32 scanlines
DUTYCYCLE             ; 32 scanlines
PULSE                 ; 34 scanlines
DUTYCYCLE             ; 32 scanlines
DUTYCYCLE             ; 32 scanlines
DUTYCYCLE             ; 32 scanlines
jmp NextFrame
```

All-in-all, this loop generates 264 scanlines while cycling the audio frequency 8 times per channel, and decrementing volume and/or loading new notes 2 times per channel.

39.1 Song File Format

Since our music player has its own lookup table, our song file doesn't need AUDC and AUDF values anymore, just the notes and their durations. Each byte of the song is either a note or a delay.

If a byte's high bit is clear, it is a note (with range 0-63). Notes are played immediately, alternating between the two channels.

If the high bit is set, the lower 7 bits are used as a delay (in 1/120 sec frames). No notes will be fetched until the delay counter expires.

The byte $FF indicates the end of the song, and the music player will start over at the beginning.

You can create song files from MIDI files using the midi2song.py script, located at http://8bitworkshop.com/tools/midi2song.py. For example:

```
# first, show the list of tracks in the MIDI file
python midi2song.py song.mid

# choose tracks 1, 2 and 4
python midi2song.py song.mid 1,2,4 -n 64 -v 2 -H
```

Timing Analysis

Since CPU timing is critical in VCS programming, you often have to count CPU cycles. If any of your loops take more than 75 cycles per iteration, you risk missing a scanline. It's even more difficult when you have multiple branches and variable-cycle instructions.

The IDE has a nifty little tool that helps you count cycles. It performs a *flow analysis* on the code, counting the cycles for each instruction it finds. For each instruction, it records the minimum and maximum number of CPU cycles from the previous STA WSYNC instruction.

You can run the flow analysis tool at any time (as long as your code assembles properly) by clicking the hourglass ⌛ button. The tool may take a few seconds to run.

For example, let's take this simple loop, similar to one we described in Chapter 5:

```
f028 9      2              ldx #192
f02a 11     3              lda BGColor
                  ScanLoop
f02c 5-14   2                adc #1
f02e 7-16   3                sta COLUBK
f030 10-19  3                sta WSYNC
f032 0      2                dex
f033 2      2                bne ScanLoop
```

If the timing column (second column from the left) is of the form "X-Y", this means that the CPU cycle count since the last WSYNC is no less than X and no more than Y. If it is of the form "X", the cycle count is exactly X.

As we see here, the instruction immediately after the STA WSYNC instruction has a cycle count of 0. This means the first cycle of the DEX instruction starts at the very beginning of a scanline. The next instruction, BNE, has a cycle count of 2, which means it is 6 color clocks into the scanline – still within the HBLANK period.

The BNE jumps back to the ScanLoop label. We see that the first instruction of that loop has a range of 5-14. The minimum value of 5 comes from the BNE instruction – 2 plus 3 cycles for the branch. The 14 comes from the instructions leading up to the loop. The flow analysis merges the two values at the branch target.

The flow analysis records values up to 152 (two scanlines) so you can analyze both one-line and two-line kernels.

41

Making Games

We've spent a lot of time on the intricacies of VCS programming and learned a lot of tricks and techniques. How do we use all that we've learned to make a full-fledged game?

Well, it's really just a manner of putting all the pieces together. Chapter 21's brick-busting game got pretty close, even though it used less than 1000 bytes of ROM.

41.1 Game Design

On the VCS, game design is largely an answer to the question "what can we do?" In other words, technical limitations drive the design.

It's common to start by mapping out the game's primary display scanline-by-scanline, accounting for players, missiles, and ball along the way. The most memorable VCS games multitasked all of the display objects – for instance, in *Pitfall!*, the player objects not only were used for the player and obstacles, but also to draw the branches of the trees overhead.

Don't forget that you can use missiles and ball to draw up to 3 vertical lines. In *Adventure*, the missiles were used as walls, and in *River Raid*, the ball was used as a fuel gauge.

It might also be wise at this point to map out the main variables you'll need in your game, since you only have 128 bytes of RAM to work with. You'll also want to account for the memory usage of RAM-hungry kernels like the ones in Chapters 23 and 26, and look at possibly sharing memory between different areas of code.

41.2   Game Programming

Now that you have the design figured out, it's just a simple matter of programming! Just use your fingers to type the keys in the correct order!

Joking aside, it's a good idea to start with a template like the skeleton NTSC frame example in Figure 12.1 (the IDE creates one automatically). It's also convenient to create subroutines where possible, like this:

```
NextFrame
        VERTICAL_SYNC
        TIMER_SETUP 37
        jsr FrameSetup
        TIMER_WAIT
        TIMER_SETUP 192
        jsr DrawFrame
        TIMER_WAIT
        TIMER_SETUP 29
        jsr FrameEnd
        TIMER_WAIT
        jmp NextFrame
```

Sometimes you don't have the extra 12 CPU cycles to spare for a JSR/RTS cycle, so it's okay to inline the code, too.

Most VCS games showed the same basic display whether or not a game was active. If you need a title screen or other wholly separate display kernels, you could duplicate the main loop entirely, or maybe just use the JMP (xx) instruction to switch between different kernels:

```
        TIMER_SETUP 192
        jmp (CurrentKernel)
BackFromKernel              ; make sure kernel jumps back here
        TIMER_WAIT
```

As usual, it's a tradeoff between shaving off a few CPU cycles, a few bytes of ROM, or making the code more readable.

Historical Note: Some games featured an "attract mode" which cycled the color palette when the game was inactive for a period of time, preventing CRT burn-in. This was usually done by EOR-ing with a slowly-changing variable before setting color registers.

41.3 Distributing Your Game

Now that you've put hours of work into your game designing, developing, playtesting, and tweaking, it's time to share it with the world!

The easiest way is to just click the "Share" button in the IDE which generates a shareable Web URL. Anyone opening this link will see the source code and be able to play the emulated game in the browser. You can also download the ROM file from the IDE and distribute it for use in other emulators like Stella.

If you want to play your game on actual hardware, there are several options. First, you have to get a console. For ultimate authenticity, you can pick up a vintage Atari VCS/2600 online. You'll need to either visit a thrift store to pick up a CRT television (recommended) or find a monitor that has a composite input.

You could also find a used Atari Flashback 2, which is a modern reinvention of the VCS that accepts external cartridges and outputs HDMI.

Now you have to get your game's ROM into the console. The easiest way is probably the Harmony Cartridge[8]. Just put your ROM on a SD or microSD card, slide it into the cartridge, and then pop the cartridge into your game console. From there you can select from available ROMs using an onscreen menu.

You could also DIY your own cartridge by programming a fast microcontroller to respond to memory requests in the same way a ROM chip would, and then building a breadboard with a cartridge slot connector. This is outside the scope of this book, but plenty of resources are available online.

Once you are satisfied with your game, you can pay for a service like AtariAge to manufacture your very own cartridge complete with a custom label.

42

Troubleshooting

When programming for the Atari, there are times when nothing seems to work no matter what you try! In this chapter, we'll list symptoms you may encounter that indicate common problems, and include tips for solving them.

Screen "flips" continuously

You are not drawing the right number of scanlines. Make sure your code draws exactly 262 scanlines by counting WSYNCs and by using the timer routines in Chapter 12. You can see the current number of scanlines by clicking the emulator window and typing Ctrl-G (Alt-G on Mac).

Screen "flips" periodically

If the screen flips only every once in a while, you might have code that misses scanlines. Make sure you don't spend more than 75 cycles before a STA WSYNC. If you are using the timer routines, you may be running past the TIMER_END macro.

Sprites or objects wiggle by one scanline

You may have forgotten to clear (CLC) the carry flag before an ADC, or set (SEC) the carry flag before a SBC. This leaves the carry flag in whatever state it was in, and thus the addition or subtraction might be off by zero or one.

Garbled sprite that changes with horizontal position

You may be writing a register too late. See if you can rearrange things so that registers are written to in the 22-CPU cycle HBLANK period.

Sprites are smeared or move quickly horizontally across the screen

You may be forgetting to reset the HMxx registers (STA HMCLR being the easiest way), so the sprites move every time HMOVE is strobed.

Setting GRPx registers has no effect

You may have set a VDEL register without realizing it, and maybe you aren't alternating writes to GRP0 and GRP1.

Timing problems

If timing isn't as consistent as you expect it to be, you may have indexed memory accesses across page boundaries (which add +1 cycle) or branches across page boundaries (which add +1 cycle).

Branches don't seem to work properly

Make sure you consult the table in Chapter 1 and that you don't have any intervening instructions that modify flags.

$ vs % vs #

Remember that $ is for hexadecimal numbers, and % is for binary numbers. Anything else is treated as a decimal number.

Also remember that unless your operand is prefixed with #, the instruction loads from memory.

Errors in include files

When using macros, errors might be flagged at the line of the include declaration instead of where the macro is invoked.

"Unresolved symbol" in macro

For some reason, DASM does not (at the time of this writing) allow forward references in macros. If you reference a label in a macro, it must be declared before the macro is invoked.

Appendix A: VCS Memory Map

Hex Addr	Name	Bits Used 76543210	Description
00	VSYNC	......x.	Vertical Sync
01	VBLANK	xx....x.	Vertical Blank / Latched Port Enable
02	WSYNC	strobe	Wait for Horizontal Blank
04	NUSIZ0	..xx.xxx	Number-size Player/Missile 0
05	NUSIZ1	..xx.xxx	Number-size Player/Missile 1
06	COLUP0	xxxxxxx.	Color – Player/Missile 0
07	COLUP1	xxxxxxx.	Color – Player/Missile 1
08	COLUPF	xxxxxxx.	Color – Playfield/Ball
09	COLUBK	xxxxxxx.	Color – Background
0A	CTRLPF	..xx.xxx	Control Playfield, Ball
0B	REFP0	....x...	Reflect Player 0
0C	REFP1	....x...	Reflect Player 1
0D	PF0	xxxx....	Playfield 0 (pixels 0-3)
0E	PF1	xxxxxxxx	Playfield 1 (pixels 4-11)
0F	PF2	xxxxxxxx	Playfield 2 (pixels 12-19)
10	RESP0	strobe	Reset Player 0
11	RESP1	strobe	Reset Player 1
12	RESM0	strobe	Reset Missile 0
13	RESM1	strobe	Reset Missile 1
14	RESBL	strobe	Reset Ball
15	AUDC0	xxxx	Audio Control Channel 0
16	AUDC1	xxxx	Audio Control Channel 1
17	AUDF0	...xxxxx	Audio Frequency Channel 0
18	AUDF1	...xxxxx	Audio Frequency Channel 1
19	AUDV0	xxxx	Audio Volume Channel 0
1A	AUDV1	xxxx	Audio Volume Channel 1
1B	GRP0	xxxxxxxx	Graphics Bitmap Player 0
1C	GRP1	xxxxxxxx	Graphics Bitmap Player 1

Hex Addr	Name	Bits Used 76543210	Description
1D	ENAM0	......x.	Enable Missile 0
1E	ENAM1	......x.	Enable Missile 1
1F	ENABL	......x.	Enable Ball
20	HMP0	xxxx....	Horizontal Motion Player 0
21	HMP1	xxxx....	Horizontal Motion Player 1
22	HMM0	xxxx....	Horizontal Motion Missile 0
23	HMM1	xxxx....	Horizontal Motion Missile 1
24	HMBL	xxxx....	Horizontal Motion Ball
25	VDELP0	x	Vertical Delay Player 0
26	VDELP1	x	Vertical Delay Player 1
27	VDELBL	x	Vertical Delay Ball
28	RESMP0	......x.	Reset Missile 0 to Player 0
29	RESMP1	......x.	Reset Missile 1 to Player 1
2A	HMOVE	strobe	Apply Horizontal Motion (fine offsets)
2B	HMCLR	strobe	Clear Horizontal Motion Registers
2C	CXCLR	strobe	Clear Collision Latches
30	CXM0P	xx......	Collision M0-P1, M0-P0
31	CXM1P	xx......	Collision M1-P0, M1-P1
32	CXP0FB	xx......	Collision P0-PF, P0-BL
33	CXP1FB	xx......	Collision P1-PF, P1-BL
34	CXM0FB	xx......	Collision M0-PF, M0-BL
35	CXM1FB	xx......	Collision M1-PF, M1-BL
36	CXBLPF	x.......	Collision BL-PF
37	CXPPMM	xx......	Collision P0-P1, M0-M1
38	INPT0	x.......	Dumped Input Port 0
39	INPT1	x.......	Dumped Input Port 1
3A	INPT2	x.......	Dumped Input Port 2
3B	INPT3	x.......	Dumped Input Port 3
3C	INPT4	x.......	Latched Input Port 4
3D	INPT5	x.......	Latched Input Port 5
80-FF	—	xxxxxxxx	128 Bytes RAM
0280	SWCHA	xxxxxxxx	Joysticks/Controllers

Hex Addr	Name	Bits Used 76543210	Description
0281	SWACNT	xxxxxxxx	Port A DDR (Data Direction Register)
0282	SWCHB	xxxxxxxx	Console Switches
0283	SWBCNT	xxxxxxxx	Port B DDR (hardwired as input)
0284	INTIM	xxxxxxxx	Timer Output
0294	TIM1T	xxxxxxxx	Set 1 Cycle Timer
0295	TIM8T	xxxxxxxx	Set 8 Cycle Timer
0296	TIM64T	xxxxxxxx	Set 64 Cycle Timer
0297	T1024T	xxxxxxxx	Set 1024 Cycle Timer

VCS Memory Map Table

Binary	Hex	Description
xxxxx0	$00	repeated playfield
xxxxx1	$01	reflected playfield
xxxx0x	$00	non-score mode
xxxx1x	$02	score mode (2 colors)
xxx0xx	$00	players have priority
xxx1xx	$04	playfield has priority
00xxxx	$00	ball size = 1 clock
01xxxx	$10	ball size = 2 clocks
10xxxx	$20	ball size = 4 clocks
11xxxx	$30	ball size = 8 clocks

Table 2: CTRLPF Register

Appendix B: VCS Colors

Hex	+0 +1	+2 +3	+4 +5	+6 +7
00	black	dim gray	dim gray	gray
10	teal	midnight blue	sea green	steel blue
20	navy	midnight blue	steel blue	steel blue
30	navy	midnight blue	steel blue	steel blue
40	dark blue	midnight blue	dark slate blue	slate blue
50	indigo	dark orchid	dark orchid	slate blue
60	purple	brown	indian red	indian red
70	maroon	brown	sienna	indian red
80	dark red	firebrick	sienna	indian red
90	maroon	saddle brown	sienna	indian red
a0	maroon	saddle brown	sienna	dark khaki
b0	dark green	dark olive green	dark olive green	dark khaki
c0	dark green	forest green	dark olive green	cadet blue
d0	dark green	forest green	sea green	cadet blue
e0	dark green	dark slate gray	dark slate gray	cadet blue
f0	navy	midnight blue	dark slate blue	steel blue

Hex	+8 +9	+10 +11	+12 +13	+14 +15
00	dark gray	silver	light silver	white smoke
10	med. turquoise	med. turquoise	turquoise	aquamarine
20	steel blue	steel blue	med. turquoise	sky blue
30	slate blue	cornflower blue	cornflower blue	light sky blue
40	slate blue	med. purple	sky blue	light sky blue
50	med. orchid	med. orchid	light steel blue	lavender
60	pale violet-red	pale violet-red	violet	light pink
70	indian red	pale violet red	dark salmon	light pink
80	indian red	dark salmon	dark salmon	light pink
90	indian red	burlywood	dark salmon	navajo white
a0	dark khaki	tan	burlywood	navajo white
b0	dark khaki	dark khaki	pale goldenrod	pale green
c0	dark seagreen	dark seagreen	light green	pale green
d0	dark seagreen	med. aquamarine	light green	aquamarine
e0	cadetblue	med. aquamarine	med. aquamarine	pale turquoise
f0	steel blue	med. aquamarine	sky blue	light sky blue

Appendix C: 6502 Opcodes

Opcode	Mnemonic	Addressing Mode	Cycles
79	ADC	aaaa,y	4+
7D	ADC	aaaa,x	4+
69	ADC	#aa	2
61	ADC	(aa,x)	6
71	ADC	(aa),y	5+
75	ADC	aa,x	4
65	ADC	aa	3
6D	ADC	aaaa	4
0B	ANC*	#aa	2
2B	ANC*	#aa	2
39	AND	aaaa,y	4+
3D	AND	aaaa,x	4+
29	AND	#aa	2
21	AND	(aa,x)	6
31	AND	(aa),y	5+
35	AND	aa,x	4
25	AND	aa	3
2D	AND	aaaa	4
8B	ANE*	#aa	0
6B	ARR*	#aa	2
0A	ASL		2
1E	ASL	aaaa,x	7
16	ASL	aa,x	6
06	ASL	aa	5
0E	ASL	aaaa	6
4B	ASR*	#aa	2
90	BCC	branch if carry clear	2++
B0	BCS	branch if carry set	2++
F0	BEQ	branch if equal	2++
24	BIT	aa	3
2C	BIT	aaaa	4
30	BMI	branch if negative	2++

Opcode	Mnemonic	Addressing Mode	Cycles
D0	BNE	branch if not equal	2++
10	BPL	branch if positive	2++
00	BRK		7
50	BVC	branch if overflow clear	2++
70	BVS	branch if overflow set	2++
18	CLC		2
D8	CLD		2
58	CLI		2
B8	CLV		2
D9	CMP	aaaa,y	4+
DD	CMP	aaaa,x	4+
C9	CMP	#aa	2
C1	CMP	(aa,x)	6
D1	CMP	(aa),y	5+
D5	CMP	aa,x	4
C5	CMP	aa	3
CD	CMP	aaaa	4
E0	CPX	#aa	2
E4	CPX	aa	3
EC	CPX	aaaa	4
C0	CPY	#aa	2
C4	CPY	aa	3
CC	CPY	aaaa	4
C3	DCP*	(aa,x)	8+
D3	DCP*	(aa),y	8+
DB	DCP*	aaaa,y	7+
DF	DCP*	aaaa,x	7+
D7	DCP*	aa,x	6+
C7	DCP*	aa	5
CF	DCP*	aaaa	6
DE	DEC	aaaa,x	7
D6	DEC	aa,x	6
C6	DEC	aa	5
CE	DEC	aaaa	3
CA	DEX		2
88	DEY		2

Opcode	Mnemonic	Addressing Mode	Cycles
59	EOR	aaaa,y	4+
5D	EOR	aaaa,x	4+
49	EOR	#aa	2
41	EOR	(aa,x)	6
51	EOR	(aa),y	5+
55	EOR	aa,x	4
45	EOR	aa	3
4D	EOR	aaaa	4
FE	INC	aaaa,x	7
F6	INC	aa,x	6
E6	INC	aa	5
EE	INC	aaaa	6
E8	INX		2
C8	INY		2
E3	ISB*	(aa,x)	8+
F3	ISB*	(aa),y	8+
FB	ISB*	aaaa,y	7+
FF	ISB*	aaaa,x	7+
F7	ISB*	aa,x	6+
E7	ISB*	aa	5
EF	ISB*	aaaa	6
4C	JMP	aaaa	3
6C	JMP	(aaaa)	5
20	JSR	aaaa	6
BB	LAS*	aaaa,y	0
BF	LAX*	aaaa,y	4+
A3	LAX*	(aa,x)	6+
B3	LAX*	(aa),y	5+
B7	LAX*	aa,y	4+
A7	LAX*	aa	3
AF	LAX*	aaaa	4
B9	LDA	aaaa,y	4+
BD	LDA	aaaa,x	4+
A9	LDA	#aa	2
A1	LDA	(aa,x)	6
B1	LDA	(aa),y	5+

Opcode	Mnemonic	Addressing Mode	Cycles
B5	LDA	aa,x	4
A5	LDA	aa	3
AD	LDA	aaaa	4
BE	LDX	aaaa,y	4+
A2	LDX	#aa	2
B6	LDX	aa,y	4
A6	LDX	aa	3
AE	LDX	aaaa	4
BC	LDY	aaaa,x	4+
A0	LDY	#aa	2
B4	LDY	aa,x	4
A4	LDY	aa	3
AC	LDY	aaaa	4
4A	LSR		2
5E	LSR	aaaa,x	7
56	LSR	aa,x	6
46	LSR	aa	5
4E	LSR	aaaa	6
AB	LXA*	#aa	0
EA	NOP		2
1C	NOP*	aaaa,x	4+
3C	NOP*	aaaa,x	4+
5C	NOP*	aaaa,x	4+
7C	NOP*	aaaa,x	4+
DC	NOP*	aaaa,x	4+
FC	NOP*	aaaa,x	4+
80	NOP*	#aa	0
82	NOP*	#aa	0
89	NOP*	#aa	0
C2	NOP*	#aa	0
E2	NOP*	#aa	0
1A	NOP*	-	0
3A	NOP*	-	0
5A	NOP*	-	0
7A	NOP*	-	0
DA	NOP*	-	0

Opcode	Mnemonic	Addressing Mode	Cycles
FA	NOP*	-	0
14	NOP*	aa,x	4
34	NOP*	aa,x	4
54	NOP*	aa,x	4
74	NOP*	aa,x	4
D4	NOP*	aa,x	4
F4	NOP*	aa,x	4
04	NOP*	aa	3
44	NOP*	aa	3
64	NOP*	aa	3
0C	NOP*	aaaa	4
19	ORA	aaaa,y	4+
1D	ORA	aaaa,x	4+
09	ORA	#aa	2
01	ORA	(aa,x)	6
11	ORA	(aa),y	5+
15	ORA	aa,x	4
05	ORA	aa	3
0D	ORA	aaaa	4
48	PHA		3
08	PHP		3
68	PLA		4
28	PLP		4
23	RLA*	(aa,x)	8+
33	RLA*	(aa),y	8+
3B	RLA*	aaaa,y	7+
3F	RLA*	aaaa,x	7+
37	RLA*	aa,x	6+
27	RLA*	aa	5
2F	RLA*	aaaa	6
2A	ROL		2
3E	ROL	aaaa,x	7
36	ROL	aa,x	6
26	ROL	aa	5
2E	ROL	aaaa	6
6A	ROR		2

Opcode	Mnemonic	Addressing Mode	Cycles
7E	ROR	aaaa,x	7
76	ROR	aa,x	6
66	ROR	aa	5
6E	ROR	aaaa	6
63	RRA*	(aa,x)	8+
73	RRA*	(aa),y	8+
7B	RRA*	aaaa,y	7+
7F	RRA*	aaaa,x	7+
77	RRA*	aa,x	6+
67	RRA*	aa	5
6F	RRA*	aaaa	6
40	RTI		6
60	RTS		6
83	SAX*	(aa,x)	6+
97	SAX*	aa,y	4+
87	SAX*	aa	3
8F	SAX*	aaaa	4
F9	SBC	aaaa,y	4+
FD	SBC	aaaa,x	4+
E9	SBC	#aa	2
EB	SBC*	#aa	0
E1	SBC	(aa,x)	6
F1	SBC	(aa),y	5+
F5	SBC	aa,x	4
E5	SBC	aa	3
ED	SBC	aaaa	4
CB	SBX*	#aa	2
38	SEC		2
F8	SED		2
78	SEI		2
93	SHA*	(aa),y	0
9F	SHA*	aaaa,y	0
9B	SHS*	aaaa,y	0
9E	SHX*	aaaa,y	0
9C	SHY*	aaaa,x	0
03	SLO*	(aa,x)	8+

Opcode	Mnemonic	Addressing Mode	Cycles
13	SLO*	(aa),y	8+
1B	SLO*	aaaa,y	7+
1F	SLO*	aaaa,x	7+
17	SLO*	aa,x	6+
07	SLO*	aa	5
0F	SLO*	aaaa	6
43	SRE*	(aa,x)	8+
53	SRE*	(aa),y	8+
5B	SRE*	aaaa,y	7+
5F	SRE*	aaaa,x	7+
57	SRE*	aa,x	6+
47	SRE*	aa	5
4F	SRE*	aaaa	6
81	STA	(aa,x)	6
91	STA	(aa),y	6
95	STA	aa,x	4
85	STA	aa	3
99	STA	aaaa,y	5
9D	STA	aaaa,x	5
8D	STA	aaaa	4
96	STX	aa,y	4
86	STX	aa	3
8E	STX	aaaa	4
94	STY	aa,x	4
84	STY	aa	3
8C	STY	aaaa	4
AA	TAX		2
A8	TAY		2
BA	TSX		2
8A	TXA		2
9A	TXS		2
98	TYA		2

Appendix D: 6502 Instruction Flags

Summary of Documented 6502 Instructions

Mnemonic	Flags Affected	Expression
ADC	NZCV	A += opr
AND	NZ	A &= opr
ASL	NZC	opr «= 1
BCC	-	branch if C==0
BCS	-	branch if C==1
BEQ	-	branch if Z==0
BIT	NZV	(A & opr); V = bit 6
BMI	-	branch if N==1
BNE	-	branch if Z==1
BRK	B	–
BVC	-	branch if V==0
BVS	-	branch if V==1
CLC	C	C = 0
CLD	D	D = 0
CLV	V	V = 0
CMP	NZC	(A - opr)
CPX	NZC	(X - opr)
CPY	NZC	(Y - opr)
DEC	NZ	opr–
DEX	NZ	X–
DEY	NZ	Y–
EOR	NZ	A ^= opr
INC	NZ	opr++
INX	NZ	X++
INY	NZ	Y++
JMP	-	PC = opr
JSR	-	push PC-1; PC = opr
LDA	NZ	A = opr
LDX	NZ	X = opr
LDY	NZ	Y = opr
LSR	NZC	A »= 1

Summary of Documented 6502 Instructions

Mnemonic	Flags Affected	Expression
NOP	-	–
PHA	-	[S–] = A
PHP	-	[S–] = P
PLA	NZ	A = [++S]
PLP	all	P = [++S]
ORA	NZ	A |= opr
ROL	NZC	A = (A«1) | C
ROR	NZC	A = (A»1) | (C*128)
SBC	NZCV	A -= opr
SEC	C	C = 1
SED	D	D = 1
STA	-	opr = A
STX	-	opr = X
STY	-	opr = Y
TAX	NZ	X = A
TAY	NZ	Y = A
TXA	NZ	A = X
TYA	NZ	A = Y
TSX	NZ	X = S
TXS	NZ	S = X

N = Negative (Sign)
Z = Zero
C = Carry
V = Overflow
D = Decimal

Summary of Illegal 6502 Instructions

Mnemonic	Flags Affected	Expression
ANC	NZC	A &= #opr
ASR	NZC	A = (A & #opr) » 1
ARR	NZCV	A = (A & #opr) » 1
DCP	NZC	(A - opr–)
ISC	NZCV	A -= opr++
LAS	NZ	A=X=S = opr & S
LAX	NZ	A=X = opr
RLA	NZC	A = (rol A) & opr
RRA	NZCV	A = (ror A) + opr
SBX	NZC	X = (A & X) - #opr
SLO	NZC	A = (A «= 1)	opr
SRE	NZC	A = (A »= 1) ôpr

N = Negative (Sign)
Z = Zero
C = Carry
V = Overflow

Appendix E: Header Files

xmacro.h

```
;-----------------------------------------------------------
; Usage: TIMER_SETUP lines
; where lines is the number of scanlines to skip (> 2).
; The timer will be set so that it expires before this number
; of scanlines. A WSYNC will be done first.

    MAC TIMER_SETUP
.lines  SET {1}
.cycles SET ((.lines * 76) - 13)
; special case for when we have two timer events in a line
; and our 2nd event straddles the WSYNC boundary
        if (.cycles % 64) < 12
                lda #(.cycles / 64) - 1
                sta WSYNC
        else
                lda #(.cycles / 64)
                sta WSYNC
        endif
        sta TIM64T
    ENDM

;-----------------------------------------------------------
; Use with TIMER_SETUP to wait for timer to complete.
; Performs a WSYNC afterwards.

    MAC TIMER_WAIT
.waittimer
        lda INTIM
        bne .waittimer
        sta WSYNC
    ENDM
```

Additional header files may be found at:
https://github.com/sehugg/dasm/blob/master/machines/atari2600/

Bibliography

[1] Brian Bagnell. *The Spectacular Rise and Fall of Commodore*, chapter MOS Technology, 1974 - 1976. Variant Press, 2005.

[2] Paulo Augusto Peccin. Javatari. http://javatari.org/.

[3] Matthew Dillon. Documentation for DASM V2.12. http://www.macs.hw.ac.uk/%7Epjbk/scholar/dasm.html.

[4] Steve Wright. Charles Sinnett and B. Watson, editors. Stella Programmer's Guide. http://www.alienbill.com/2600/101/docs/stella.html.

[5] Kirk Israel. playerpal 2600 v2.1. http://www.alienbill.com/2600/playerpalnext.html.

[6] Kirk Israel. webTune2600 - a GUI for tune2600. http://alienbill.com/2600/basic/music/tune2600.html.

[7] Kevin Horton. Mostly Inclusive Atari 2600 Mapper / Selected Hardware Document. http://blog.kevtris.org/blogfiles/Atari%202600%20Mappers.txt.

[8] Fred Quimby. Harmony Cartridge. http://harmony.atariage.com/Site/Harmony.html.

Index

Made in the USA
Middletown, DE
02 July 2024

56685922R00146